family FÜN

CAPE TOWN, DURBAN, JOBURG & PRETORIA

Child magazine™

JOBURG, CAPE TOWN, DURBAN AND PRETORIA'S BEST GUIDE FOR PARENTS

Introduction

If you are looking for fun and interesting things to do with your family in Cape Town, Durban, Johannesburg or Pretoria, then this is the book for you. Within the confines of a limited page count, we have rounded up as many highlights in these four cities as possible, to bring you an abundance of places to visit, complete with listings of nearby attractions, shops, restaurants and places of play. This book is sure to provide you and your family with a resource of fabulous places where special memories can be made.

The *Child magazine* team is passionate about making the most of living in the city and I trust that we, with our many years of research, have sought out gems for you, whether you are a local or a tourist. I also hope that, after a few pages, you will share the sentiment of a *Child magazine* reader who once told me: 'I love your mag; it's like my cellphone – I don't know how I managed before it!' Being a tourist in your own town, or visiting from faraway lands, is always much more fun with children in tow. So we have filled these pages with fun things for children to do, from tiny tots through to the early teenager, with the added bonus of a nearby treat for you, the moms, dads, grannies and grandpas. We've made it our job – one we really do love – to let you in on sometimes little-known highlights, so that you too can experience the diversity our cities have to offer families.

Being a busy parent of two children, I'm all for things that will make parenting a little easier and a lot more fun. That's one of the main reasons I launched a practical parenting magazine in 2004, which has grown into the trusted title parents rely on today. The magazine's reach has since spread from Cape Town to Johannesburg, Durban and Pretoria, and our website receives visitors from all over the country and beyond. These parents are all looking for the same thing – fresh, honest, user-friendly content. And that's what the *Child magazine* team is dedicated to giving our readers every issue, from well-researched articles on health and education issues to entertaining, educational outings for the whole family.

It is extremely satisfying to extend the opportunity of these experiences to an audience beyond our magazine readership via this book and trust you have fun visiting some of the places we have covered.

About *Child magazine*:
Child magazine is South Africa's largest parenting magazine, with a monthly circulation of almost 183,000 copies. It is distributed free to schools in Cape Town, Durban, Johannesburg and Pretoria and is aimed at parents of children from birth to 13 years old. Health, education and entertainment are the cornerstones of *Child magazine*. You can also find us online at www.childmag.co.za

Lisa Mc Namara
Publisher, *Child magazine*

Directory of Activities

Cape Town
Central Cape Town

Getting around Cape Town

There are many reliable ways to move around the Mother City. You can go by bus, with the MyCiTi system taking you through the City Bowl, out towards the West Coast as far as Atlantis, and to Century City. Metrorail offers dependable transportation, with one of the most useful routes being the southern line, which runs from Cape Town Station, stopping at most of the southern suburbs until it reaches Simon's Town. The hop-on, hop-off City Sightseeing bus gets you to Cape Town's tourist hotspots, and you can catch any one of the ever-available taxi cabs you'll see along the high streets (Cape Town also offers the easy-to-use Uber). Fly solo with a car rental company, or organise a shuttle service from the city to the Winelands and even the Garden Route. Cape Town also has its own drop-and-go cycle service, with stations at central points.

Together with the South African Police Service (SAPS), uniformed members of the Central City Improvement District (CCID) man the streets to keep the City Bowl secure. However, as you amble along the city's vibrant streets, do your best to fly under the radar by remaining nondescript. State-of-the-art camera equipment slung around your neck is bait for opportunists.

Transport line (MyCiTi and Metrorail)
0800 656 463

Road
Taxi cabs
Uber (download the app)
www.uber.com
Excite Taxis
021 448 4444
www.excitetaxis.co.za
Intercab
021 447 7799
www.intercab.co.za
Rikkis Taxis
021 447 3559
www.rikkis.co.za

Car rentals
Europcar
011 479 4000
www.europcar.co.za
Bidvest Car Rental
086 101 7722
www.bidvestcarrental.co.za
Around About Cars
021 422 4022
www.aroundaboutcars.com

Shuttle service
Bettina Shuttle
(for shuttle services to the Cape Peninsula, Winelands and even the Garden Route)
021 887 0702
www.bettinashuttle.co.za

Tour
City Sightseeing Cape Town
021 511 6000
www.citysightseeing.co.za

Rail
Shosholoza Meyl
(for long-distance trips between Joburg, Cape Town and/or Durban)
086 000 8888
www.shosholozameyl.co.za
Metrorail Western Cape
www.capemetrorail.co.za

Central Cape Town

1. Atlantic Rail steam train
2. Bree Street
3. Camps Bay
4. Cape Town City Sightseeing
5. Castle of Good Hope
6. Clifton's four beaches
7. De Waal Park
8. Deer Park Nature Reserve
9. District Six Museum
10. Green Point Urban Park
11. Iziko South African Museum and Planetarium
12. Lion's Head
13. Noon Day Gun walk
14. Oranjezicht City Farm market
15. Rhodes Memorial
16. Sea Point Promenade and Pavilion
17. Table Mountain Aerial Cableway
18. The Blue Train Park
19. The Company's Gardens
20. Tunnel Tours with Good Hope Adventures
21. Two Oceans Aquarium
22. V&A Waterfront shopping destination
23. Zip Zap Circus shows

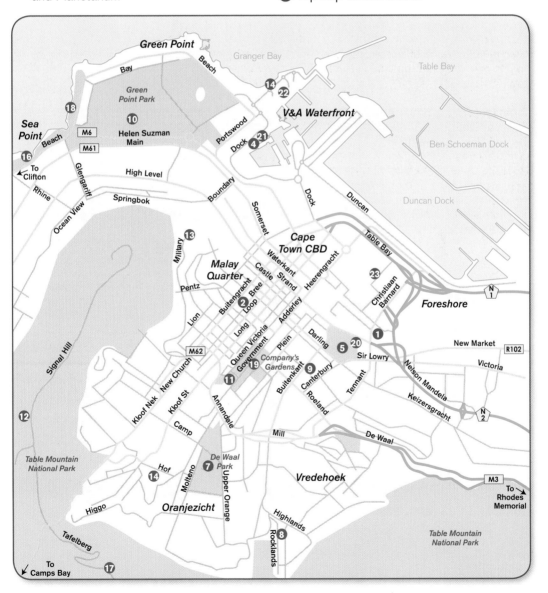

1 Atlantic Rail steam train
www.atlanticrail.co.za

 5/5 Party venue rating
 3/5 Rainy day option

Why not take family and friends on a vintage steam train ride? The scenic route begins in Cape Town, winding along the False Bay coast to arrive at Simon's Town, and at the Winelands on select Sundays.

Address	Train Lodge Hotel, Foreshore
GPS marker	33°55'27"S; 18°25'53"E
Closest public transport	Cape Town Railway Station, Metrorail
Opening hours	9:30am or 10:30am–5pm day trips
Most appropriate age group	3+
Pram/wheelchair-friendly	Yes for prams, no for wheelchairs
Baby-changing facility	No
Nearest hospital	Netcare Christiaan Barnard Memorial Hospital, 021 480 6111

Take note:
Don't go to Cape Town Station for the departure. Visit the website for directions to the Train Lodge Hotel.

COST R200 for 3–12-year-olds, R300 per adult

Nearby
Visit/see: Artscape Theatre, DF Malan Street, Foreshore, 021 410 9800 (theatre) or 021 421 7695 (booking line).
Shop: Food Lover's Market, Hans Strijdom Avenue, 021 425 2814.

---

2 Bree Street

 1/5 Party venue rating
 4/5 Rainy day option

The Bree Street strip has built up its vibrant street cred by attracting only the most interesting cafés, a barber, boutiques and galleries. With a bakery, bagel bar or even a bacon bar (that all open early) on pretty much every corner, this street is best explored on foot, hand-in-hand with your Curious George.

 COST Varies per venue

Take note:
Look out for Richard Bosman's Bacon Bar.

Address	Bree Street, CBD
GPS marker	33°55'32"S; 18°24'48"E
Closest public transport	MyCiTi bus route 101, 106, 107
Opening hours	Vary per venue
Most appropriate age group	7+
Pram/wheelchair-friendly	Yes
Baby-changing facility	No
Nearest hospital	Netcare Christiaan Barnard Memorial Hospital, 021 480 6111

Special event
The Little Maestros classical concerts take place on the second Tuesday of every month at the YoungBlood Collective

3 Camps Bay
www.campsbayinfo.com

3/5 Party venue rating
0/5 Rainy day option

Clifton 6 — Kloof — Table Mountain National Park
M6 — Victoria — M62
Camps Bay 3 — Camps Bay

Tucked beneath the Twelve Apostles and Lion's Head lies a trendy beachside suburb. On a sunny day, get to Camps Bay early to nab a parking spot, grab a coffee and slowly stroll the length of the palm tree-lined promenade in the direction of Hout Bay as your children dart between you and the sand with their spades and buckets. Once you've walked the length of the strip you can all cool off at the saltwater rock pool. It's great for children as there is no need to worry about waves.

Address	Victoria Road, Camps Bay
GPS marker	33°57'04"S; 18°22'42"E
Closest public transport	MyCiTi bus route 106 or 107
Most appropriate age group	6+
Pram/wheelchair-friendly	Yes
Baby-changing facility	No
Nearest hospital	Mediclinic Cape Town, 021 464 5500

Nearby
Eat: Col'Cacchio, corner Victoria Road and The Meadway, 021 438 2171.
Primi Piatti, Brighton Court, Victoria Road, 021 438 9149.
Grand Café, Victoria Road, 021 438 4253.
For parents: Theatre on the Bay, Link Street, 021 438 3301.

4 Cape Town City Sightseeing

www.citysightseeing.co.za

The open-top double-decker hop-on hop-off buses are one of the best ways for families to take in more than 20 of Cape Town's iconic attractions and destinations. The red route stops at the Two Oceans Aquarium, V&A Waterfront, the Iziko South African Museum and Table Mountain Cableway, with a route that explores the city's downtown section. The blue route covers Kirstenbosch National Botanical Garden, Camps Bay, Sea Point, Imizamo Yethu Township and Hout Bay, with the wine-tour part of the journey stopping at Groot Constantia, Beau Constantia and Eagles' Nest wine estates. There is also a night tour, which stops to picnic at Signal Hill between September and April; township tours exploring Langa and Gugulethu; a walking tour of Cape Town and Bo-Kaap, and a water taxi through the waterfront canals. There is commentary in 16 languages, and children get their own 'kids' channel' along with a free activity book.

Tel number	0861 733 287 or 021 511 6000
Address	Dock Road, V&A Waterfront
GPS marker	33°54'27"S; 18°25'03"E
Closest public transport	MyCiTi bus route 104
Opening hours	9am–5pm
Most appropriate age group	5+
Pram/wheelchair-friendly	Yes
Baby-changing facility	No
Nearest hospital	Somerset Hospital, 021 402 6911

COST One-day ticket is free for children under 5 years old, R80 for 5–17-year-olds and R170 per adult

⑤ Castle of Good Hope
www.castleofgoodhope.co.za

3/5 Party venue rating

4/5 Rainy day option

Visiting the oldest building in South Africa with the family is a fascinating step back in time to Cape Town's origins. Tours are available throughout the day. Visit the Castle Military Museum and see a replica of a forge and how it operated in the 17th and 18th centuries. Learn about the original castle, and how it has been restored and changed, and see the soldiers perform their military duties, including the key ceremony. There are horse-and-carriage rides available from this destination (082 575 5669).

Tel number	021 787 1260
Address	Corner Darling and Buitenkant streets, CBD
GPS marker	33°55'32"S; 18°25'37"E
Closest public transport	Cape Town Railway Station, Metrorail, and MyCiTi bus route 103
Opening hours	9am–4pm daily
Most appropriate age group	7+
Pram/wheelchair-friendly	Yes
Baby-changing facility	No
Nearest hospital	Groote Schuur Hospital, 021 404 9111
	Mediclinic Cape Town, 021 464 5500

Special event
The Military Tattoo

COST: Adults R30, children/pensioners R15 Monday to Saturday; Adults R25, children/pensioners R10 Sunday

⑥ Clifton's four beaches

4/5 Party venue rating

0/5 Rainy day option

Clifton is an exclusive residential area that is home to a Blue Flag beach that has been rated among the top 10 in the world. The four wind-protected beaches are each separated by a rocky outcrop and are popular for swimming, surfing, stand-up paddleboarding, and endless games of bat and ball. They are named First Beach, Second Beach, Third Beach and Fourth Beach – each of them characterised by their white sand and cold water. Being in one of the most up-market suburbs of Cape Town, a classic view from your spot on the sand is of yachts floating close to shore. Fourth Beach, with its Blue Flag status, is the perfect family beach, with clean facilities, somewhere to buy cold drinks and snacks, umbrellas and deck chairs to hire and a lifeguard presence. If it gets too busy, you can quite easily walk across to the quieter beaches.

Address	All four beaches are located along Victoria Road
GPS marker	33°56'31"S; 18°22'31"E
Closest public transport	MyCiTi bus route 108, 109
Most appropriate age group	6+
Pram/wheelchair-friendly	No
Baby-changing facility	No
Nearest hospital	Somerset Hospital, 021 402 6911

Nearby
Eat: The Bungalow Restaurant, Victoria Road, Clifton, 021 438 2018.

Special event
Moonstruck Summer Beach Concert on Fourth Beach

Take note:
The Clifton beaches can only be accessed from the street by steep walkways, although Fourth offers the easiest access.

7 De Waal Park
www.dewaalpark.co.za

5/5 Party venue rating

0/5 Rainy day option

In the middle of the City Bowl lies a beautiful green space for children, dogs, picnickers, slackliners, birders and runners. Run Rabbit Run Coffee Roastery has set up in the bandstand over weekends. In the past, the Friends of De Waal Park have organised free concerts in the park in summer, so keep your eyes open for advertisements on street posters.

Address	Upper Orange Street, Oranjezicht, City Bowl
GPS marker	33°56'11"S; 18°24'45"E
Closest public transport	MyCiTi bus route 103
Opening hours	6:30am–8pm September to March, 7am–6pm April to August
Most appropriate age group	2+
Pram/wheelchair-friendly	Yes
Baby-changing facility	No
Nearest hospital	Mediclinic Cape Town, 021 464 5500

Nearby

Eat: Pulp Kitchen, Gardens Shopping Centre, corner Mill and Buitenkant streets, Gardens, 021 462 5691.

Shop: Polly Potter's Toy Store, Gardens Shopping Centre, 021 461 0579.

 Deer Park Nature Reserve

www.tmnp.co.za

This green belt is found at the end of a long road that stretches into the mountain – it is literally a stone's throw from the City Bowl. Picnic, hike, cycle and explore with the family in abundant surrounds featuring fynbos, succulents, towering trees, leafy paths, a gently flowing stream, small mountain pools, chirping birds and views of a dwarfed City Bowl on one side and Table Mountain rising overwhelmingly on the other. The reserve is a favourite for dog walkers with permits, and there are some great MTB trails to be explored. You can go on an easy meander or a more challenging climb; if you just want to explore the wooden paths, you can get away with wearing slip-slops. The picnic area offers concrete tables and chairs, or you can simply set up under a welcoming tree. No braaiing facilities.

Address	Access the reserve from Rocklands Avenue, Vredehoek
GPS marker	33°56'48"S; 18°25'12"E
Closest public transport	MyCiTi bus route 103
Most appropriate age group	1+
Pram/wheelchair-friendly	Yes
Baby-changing facility	No
Nearest hospital	Mediclinic Cape Town, 021 464 5500

Nearby

Eat: Deer Park Café, Deer Park Drive, 021 462 6311.

For parents: Woodlands Eatery, Deer Park Drive, 021 801 5799. Con Brio Bistro, Deer Park Drive, 021 461 9957.

District Six Museum

9

www.districtsix.co.za

This museum preserves important Cape history as it recounts the time, in 1966, when the apartheid government swooped in on District Six to forcibly remove the locals and declare the area a 'whites-only' zone. As part of the City Sightseeing red route, the family can easily incorporate the museum into a day trip as one of their cultural explorations. A highlight would be to book a guided tour with an ex-resident through the streets of District Six.

Tel number	021 466 7200
Address	Buitenkant Street, CBD
GPS marker	33°55'40"S; 18°25'25"E
Closest public transport	MyCiTi bus route 103
Opening hours	9am–4pm Monday to Saturday
Most appropriate age group	7+
Pram/wheelchair-friendly	Yes
Baby-changing facility	No
Nearest hospital	Mediclinic Cape Town, 021 464 5500

COST: R30 per adult for a self-guided visit, R45 per person for an ex-resident guide, R5 per scholar

Nearby

Visit/see: The Book Lounge, Roeland Street, 021 462 2425.

Eat: Downtown Ramen, Harrington Street, 021 461 0407 (no bookings, only walk-ins). Truth Café, Buitenkant Street, 021 200 0440.

Shop: Charly's Bakery, Canterbury Street, Zonnebloem, 021 461 5181. Tinka Tonka Toys, Buitenkant Street, Gardens, 021 461 1441.

For parents: The Fugard, corner Caledon and Lower Buitenkant streets, District Six, 021 461 4554.

Special event

Open Book Festival

10 Green Point Urban Park
www.capetownstadium.capetown.gov.za

5/5
Party venue rating

0/5
Rainy day option

This incredible green space is a favourite among local families. The park offers picnic spots, a biodiversity showcase garden, informal outdoor celebrations, a wetland garden, walking and cycling paths, an outdoor exercise gym, a tot-lot playpark for children 1–6 years old, an adventure playpark for children 7–16 years old, and an outdoor labyrinth. Dogs are welcome but must be leashed at all times. You can book a visit to Cape Town Stadium for one of their educational tours. You will feel safe with the presence of security personnel who patrol the park and are stationed at all the entrances.

Tel number	021 417 0120
Address	Cape Town Stadium, Green Point
GPS marker	33°54'15"S; 18°24'04"E
Closest public transport	MyCiTi bus route 104
Opening hours	7am–7pm daily
Most appropriate age group	2+
Pram/wheelchair-friendly	Yes
Baby-changing facility	Yes
Nearest hospital	Somerset Hospital, 021 402 6911

Nearby
Visit/see: Cape Sidecar Adventures, Glengariff Road, Green Point, 021 434 9855.
Play/do: Artjamming, V&A Waterfront (above Toy Kingdom), 021 421 6129.
Eat: 65 on Main, Main Road, Green Point, 021 439 9559. The Banting Kitchen, Main Road, Green Point, 021 430 0506 (for Banting options). NU Health Food Café, Main Road, Sea Point, 021 439 7269. Franky's Diner, Main Road, Sea Point, 021 433 0445.
Shop: Cape Quarter Lifestyle Village, Somerset Road, Green Point, 021 421 1111. Kids Emporium, Somerset Square Road, Green Point, 021 418 7636. Giovanni's Deli, Main Road, Green Point, 021 434 6893.
Sleep: Cape Royale Hotel, Main Road, Green Point, 021 430 0500.

11 Iziko South African Museum and Planetarium

www.iziko.org.za

5/5 Party venue rating

5/5 Rainy day option

The fascinating natural history collections feature marine biology, invertebrates and vertebrates, Karoo palaeontology and dioramas as well as rocks and minerals. In the museum's natural history programme children learn according to their age group about everything from fossils and sea life to reptiles, mammals, archaeology and the universe. Throughout the year, planetarium shows feature an age-appropriate guide to the night sky and our universe in the celestial theatre. There is an activity room for children over school holidays, offering robotics workshops for various age groups as well as free art and natural history workshops. The museum also collaborates on fun, innovative community activities such as Museum Night.

Tel number	021 481 3800/3900
Address	25 Queen Victoria Street, CBD
GPS marker	33°55'41"S; 18°24'55"E
Closest public transport	MyCiTi bus route 101
Opening hours	10am–5pm daily
Most appropriate age group	6+
Pram/wheelchair-friendly	Yes
Baby-changing facility	Yes, at the museum
Nearest hospital	Mediclinic Cape Town, 021 464 5500 or Netcare Christiaan Barnard Memorial Hospital, 021 480 6111

COST Adults R30–R40, 6–18 years old R15–R20, SA students and pensioners R15–R20, family ticket (two adults and two children) R75, under 5 free

Nearby

Visit/see: South African Jewish Museum and its restaurant, Hatfield Street, 021 465 1546.

Play/do: Gardens Skate Park, Mill Street bridge, Gardens.

Eat: Café Riteve, Hatfield Street, 021 465 1594. Dunkley Square restaurants: Maria's for Greek cuisine, 021 461 3333; Vandiar's Indian Cuisine, 021 462 6129; and Aubergine for fine dining, 021 465 0000.

Special event

Wildlife Photographer of the Year Exhibition

12 Lion's Head

www.tmnp.co.za

2/5 Party venue rating

0/5 Rainy day option

The popular walk to the top of Lion's Head takes about three hours and can be rather challenging, with many tackling the walk during full moon. On your walk around the mountain you'll get 360° views of the Mother City and Table Bay on one side, and the Atlantic shoreline on the other. Many outdoorsy families enjoy the walk with their young children harnessed onto their backs. Lion's Head is also a great spot to go paragliding, hang-gliding or microlighting when Signal Hill is not being used. Get your hands on the book *Lion's Head Hunt*, in *The Young Explorers* series by Suzie Joubert.

Address	Access via Kloof Nek Road
GPS marker	33°56'13"S; 18°23'41"E
Closest public transport	City Sightseeing bus red route
Most appropriate age group	9+
Pram/wheelchair-friendly	No
Baby-changing facility	No
Nearest hospital	Mediclinic Cape Town, 021 464 5500

13 Noon Day Gun walk

0/5
Party venue rating

0/5
Rainy day option

Take the family on a walk through Bo-Kaap, from the corner of Bloem and Buitengracht streets via Military Road to the Lion Battery where the cannons are situated. Get there by 11:30am to watch the daily ritual and hear an interesting talk about Cape Town's oldest living tradition – the 'firing' of the cannons at noon exactly.

Address	Lion Battery, Signal Hill
GPS marker	33°54'55"S; 18°24'41"E
Closest public transport	MyCiTi bus route 101
Most appropriate age group	8+
Opening hours	Arrive by 11:30am for a presentation
Pram/wheelchair-friendly	No
Baby-changing facility	No
Nearest hospital	Netcare Christiaan Barnard Memorial Hospital, 021 480 6111

Nearby
Eat: Bo-Kaap Kombuis, August Street, Schotsche Kloof, 021 422 5446.
Shop: Atlas Trading, Wale Street, Schotsche Kloof, 021 423 4361.
For parents: Fireman's Arms, corner Buitengracht and Mechau streets, 021 419 1513.

14 Oranjezicht City Farm market

www.ozcf.co.za/market-day

0/5 Party venue rating **2/5** Rainy day option

This is a bustling community market that literally takes over the suburb of Higgovale every Saturday. Independent local farmers and artisanal food producers sell items for your weekly grocery shop. The market is designed to inspire you to build an alternative food system by selling edible plants and seedlings, compost, and gardening supplies and equipment. It caters for vegans and vegetarians, raw foodies, and customers who want wheat-, gluten-, sugar- and dairy-free alternatives. Children can enjoy storytelling, planting, craft, yoga and more. Picnic blankets and well-behaved dogs are welcome.

Address	Leeuwenhof Garden Estate, Hof Street (winter location at Granger Bay, V&A Waterfront)
GPS marker	33°56'14"S; 18°24'26"E
Closest public transport	MyCiTi bus route103
Opening hours	9am–2pm every Saturday
Most appropriate age group	3+
Pram/wheelchair-friendly	Yes
Baby-changing facility	No
Nearest hospital	Mediclinic Cape Town, 021 464 5500

Nearby

Visit/see: Oranjezicht City Farm, Homestead Park, Upper Orange Street, 083 628 3426 or 083 508 1066.
Eat: Café Paradiso (children can make their own pizza or biscuits), Kloof Street, 021 423 8653.
Shop: Wellness Warehouse, Lifestyle on Kloof, Kloof Street, Gardens, 021 487 5420.
Sleep: The Cape Colonial, Union Street, Gardens, 083 529 5149.
For parents: The Bombay Bicycle Club, Kloof Street, Gardens, 021 423 6805.

Take note:
You can pick your own harvest on the first Wednesday of each month at the farm in Homestead Park.

15 Rhodes Memorial

www.rhodesmemorial.co.za

3/5 Party venue rating **3/5** Rainy day option

This historic spot in Cape Town, just below Devil's Peak, has a lovely shaded play area among the trees and is a family favourite. Parents can enjoy the view while children play. The Rhodes Memorial site is a base for many scenic hikes, and the restaurant offers casual, alfresco dining.

Tel number	021 687 0000 or 082 494 5505 or 078 820 5577
Address	Groote Schuur Estate, Devil's Peak
GPS marker	33°57'09"S; 18°27'34"E
Closest public transport	Rondebosch Railway Station, Metrorail
Opening hours	9am–5pm daily
Most appropriate age group	6+
Pram/wheelchair-friendly	Yes, limited
Baby-changing facility	Yes, at the Rhodes Memorial Restaurant
Nearest hospital	Mediclinic Cape Town, 021 464 5500

Nearby

<u>Visit/see</u>: The Heart of Cape Town Museum, Groote Schuur Hospital, Old Main Building, Groote Schuur Drive, Observatory, 021 404 1967.

<u>Eat</u>: Rhodes Memorial Restaurant, Groote Schuur Estate, 021 687 0000.

<u>For parents</u>: Devil's Peak Brewery, Cecil Road, Salt River, 021 200 5818.

---

16   Sea Point Promenade and Pavilion

www.capetown.gov.za

4/5 Party venue rating   **1/5** Rainy day option

The promenade is a special city space for cyclists, skateboarders, joggers and strollers in the early morning or after work. There are a number of children's playgrounds dotted along the promenade, as well as a sea-water swimming pool complex at the Sea Point Pavilion, which has two children's pools, a diving pool and an Olympic-sized pool. The water in the pool is warmer than the ocean, making it hugely popular. The paved strip that runs alongside Beach Road between Bantry Bay and Mouille Point puts you in direct contact with the refreshing, cool ocean breeze.

COST R10.50 per child and R21 per adult for the swimming pool

Tel number	021 434 3341
Address	Beach Road, Sea Point
GPS marker	33°55'08"S; 18°23'04"E
Closest public transport	MyCiTi bus route 108 or 109
Opening hours	The promenade is open all the time and the swimming pool pavilion is open 9am–5pm in winter and 7am–7pm in summer
Most appropriate age group	4+
Pram/wheelchair-friendly	Yes, for the pavilion and promenade
Baby-changing facility	Yes, the pavilion is equipped
Nearest hospital	Somerset Hospital, 021 402 6911

Nearby

Visit/see: Sea Point Library (for story time called Pram Jam every Wednesday), 021 439 7440.
Play/do: Up Cycles Drop-and-Go Bike Rental Company, The Pavilion on the Sea Point Promenade, 076 135 2223, 074 100 9161.
Eat: Posticino's, Main Road, Sea Point, 021 439 4014.

Special event

Sea Point Promenade is the site for many well-known fun runs, especially The Color Run

Take note:
You may notice building obstructions at certain points of the promenade. This will continue as part of the city's upgrade of the public space, which is set to be completed by 2017.

---

 17 **Table Mountain Aerial Cableway**

www.tablemountain.net

 5/5 Party venue rating

 1/5 Rainy day option

Table Mountain National Park · Higgo · Tafelberg · To Camps Bay · 14 · 17

Spend a day out with the family on the iconic Table Mountain, one of the New 7 Wonders of Nature, enjoying panoramic views of Cape Town, Robben Island, the Peninsula and beyond. Take the five-minute cable-car trip to the top of Table Mountain to explore the summit; the cable car floor rotates, giving everyone a 360° view of the city. The children will love seeing the dassies scuttling along the rocks and the lizards sunning themselves. The three visitor walks along the top of the mountain are neither long nor strenuous, are on level ground and are easy to navigate. If the children are early risers, the Cableway's extended operating hours in summer will allow you to catch the first cable car up at 8am. There is a restaurant at the top of the mountain offering full meals, as well as a small shop where you can pick up a snack and a postcard. If you are feeling adventurous, you could abseil down a cliff face with Abseil Africa, suitable for children weighing at least 40kg (this is for the average 12-year-old).

Tel number	021 424 0015
Address	Tafelberg Road
GPS marker	33°56'54"S; 18°24'11"E
Closest public transport	City Sightseeing bus red route
Opening hours	Varies according to month and season (visit the website)
Most appropriate age group	4+
Pram/wheelchair-friendly	Yes
Baby-changing facility	Yes
Nearest hospital	Mediclinic Cape Town, 021 464 5500

Nearby
Eat: The Roundhouse, Roundhouse Road, Camps Bay, 021 438 4347.

COST
R110 for 4–17-year-olds, R225 per adult and R95 per pensioner

---

18 The Blue Train Park
www.thebluetrainpark.com

5/5 Party venue rating
0/5 Rainy day option

A genuine paradise for children; it is centrally located and therefore attracts families from all parts of the city. Among the many things for children to enjoy are the miniature blue train, climbing rock, large and small outdoor climbing jungle gym, a basketball court, various obstacles, a mini oval bike track, a push-bike dirt track for toddlers, seesaws, a 7.5m adventure slide, mini zip line and an outdoor art studio. The park is situated alongside the Promenade and is enclosed.

COST
R15 each

Tel number	084 314 9200
Address	Beach Road, Mouille Point
GPS marker	33°54'10"S; 18°23'56"E
Closest public transport	MyCiTi bus route 104 or 105
Opening hours	9:30am–6pm, Tuesday to Sunday; reduced hours in winter
Most appropriate age group	2–9
Pram/wheelchair-friendly	Yes
Baby-changing facility	No
Nearest hospital	Somerset Hospital, 021 402 6911

Nearby

Visit/see: Green Point Lighthouse, Beach Road, Mouille Point, 021 449 5171.
Play/do: Sea kayaking, Kaskazi Kayak, Beach Road, 021 439 1134, 083 346 1146.
Eat: La Vie, Beach Road, Sea Point, 021 433 1530.
For parents: Winchester Mansions' jazz brunch or cocktails at sunset, Beach Road, Sea Point, 021 434 2351.

---

19 **The Company's Gardens**
www.capetown.gov.za

4/5
Party venue rating

2/5
Rainy day option

Take the children for a stroll along the leafy Government Avenue to explore this park and heritage site in central Cape Town. It has a koi fish pond; rose, vegetable, Japanese, herb and rockery gardens; an aviary, and historic statues. The busy pigeons, Egyptian geese, ducks and squirrels will entertain your children (you're allowed to feed them). This venue honours its rich history with plaques throughout the garden, and interesting self-guided walks are possible. The Company's Gardens Restaurant is a fantastic outdoor eatery for families, with a play area for children.

Take note:
The entire Company's Gardens area is a Wi-Fi zone.

Tel number	021 426 1357/1218/1768
Address	19 Queen Victoria Street, CBD
GPS marker	33°55'42"S; 18°24'59"E
Closest public transport	Cape Town Railway Station, Metrorail
Opening hours	7am–7pm, and from December to February 7am–8pm
Most appropriate age group	2+
Pram/wheelchair-friendly	Yes
Baby-changing facility	No
Nearest hospital	Mediclinic Cape Town, 021 464 5500

Take note:
Free concerts are often hosted over important South African public holidays such as Human Rights Day (21 March), so be sure to watch the press for details.

20 Tunnel Tours with Good Hope Adventures

www.goodhopeadventures.com

Meet with the family at the Castle of Good Hope and explore the secret tunnels beneath the surface of Cape Town's City Bowl. These tours last between one and three hours and follow the course of the river that runs from Table Mountain to the Castle of Good Hope. Parts of the underground canals date back to 1652.

Tel number	021 510 7517 or 082 482 4006
Address	Castle of Good Hope, CBD
GPS marker	33°55'32"S; 18°25'37"E
Closest public transport	Cape Town Railway Station, Metrorail or MyCiTi bus route 103
Opening hours	By arrangement
Most appropriate age group	7+
Pram/wheelchair-friendly	No
Baby-changing facility	No
Nearest hospital	Mediclinic Cape Town, 021 464 5500

Nearby

Visit/see: Central Library, Drill Hall, Darling Street, 021 467 1567. Cape Town free walking tour with Nielsen Tours, corner of Burg and Shortmarket streets, 076 636 9007.

Eat: Col'Cacchio, Hans Strijdom Avenue, 021 419 4848, and Frères Bistro, Hans Strijdom Avenue, 021 418 1609 (both to be found in Chiappini Square). Eastern Food Bazaar, Longmarket Street, 021 461 2458. The Company's Garden Restaurant, Queen Victoria Road, 021 423 2919. Jason Bakery, Bree Street, 021 424 5644. Café Frank, Bree Street, 021 423 0360. Bocca, corner Bree and Wale streets, 021 422 0188.

Shop: Adderley Street for a variety of shops and the flower market. The Earth Fair Market on Thursdays, St George's Mall. The City Bowl Market on Hope on Thursday evenings, Gardens.

Sleep: The Rooftop Airstream Trailer Park at The Grand Daddy Hotel, Long Street, 021 424 7247.

For parents: Fork Tapas Bar, Long Street, 021 424 6334. The Crypt (for live jazz), St George's Cathedral, Wale Street, 079 683 4658.

Special event

First Thursdays

COST: Between R175 and R350 per person

21 **Two Oceans Aquarium**
www.aquarium.co.za

There are many fun ways to view the more than 3,000 marine creatures at one of the finest aquariums in the world. At the I&J Predator Exhibit you can see ragged-tooth sharks and stingrays and even dive in the aquarium and get close to the sharks and shoals of other large predators. The Penguin Exhibit begins with a journey of a typical Western Cape river from its mouth at the ocean to its origins as a stream high up in the mountains, and boasts a breeding colony of African and rockhopper penguins. The Kelp Forest Exhibit is an underwater forest that is home to shoals of silver fish. The Afrisam Children's Centre runs puppet shows, face painting and supervised art and craft activities for children between four and 10 years old. The Touch Pool is a hands-on interaction with kelp, starfish, anemones and hermit crabs overseen by guides with interesting facts to share. The Microscope Exhibit zooms you into the feeding, breathing and birth habits of goose barnacles, cushion stars and sea cucumbers. Meet the rockhopper in a penguin encounter and view shark feeds on Sunday afternoons.

Tel number	021 418 3823
Address	Dock Road, V&A Waterfront
GPS marker	33°54'27"S; 18°25'03"E
Closest public transport	MyCiTi bus route 104
Opening hours	9:30am–6pm daily
Most appropriate age group	4+
Pram/wheelchair-friendly	Yes
Baby-changing facility	Yes
Nearest hospital	Somerset Hospital, 021 402 6911

COST
R63 for 4–13-year-olds,
R102 for 14–17-year-olds,
R131 for adults,
children under 4 free

22 V&A Waterfront shopping destination

5/5 Party venue rating

5/5 Rainy day option

www.waterfront.co.za

From the Watershed, which is a craft and design market that offers children's activities over school holidays, the Cape Wheel and the V&A Food Market, with its play area upstairs, to Robben Island and an amphitheatre offering various performances over the holidays, there is plenty for the family to do. There are two play areas, one next to the amphitheatre and one at the Clock Tower.

Tel number	021 408 7500
Address	V&A Waterfront, Breakwater Boulevard
GPS marker	33°54'17"S; 18°25'12"E
Closest public transport	MyCiTi bus route 104
Opening hours	9am–9pm daily
Most appropriate age group	1+
Pram/wheelchair-friendly	Yes
Baby-changing facility	Yes
Nearest hospital	Somerset Hospital, 021 402 6911

Nearby

Visit/see: The Cape Wheel, V&A Waterfront, 021 418 2502. The Market on the Wharf, V&A Waterfront. Oceana Power Boat Club, Beach Road, Granger Bay, 021 419 1322. Galloway Theatre, Port Road, 021 418 4600. The Springbok Experience Rugby Museum, Portswood Road, 021 418 4741.
Play/do: Jolly Roger Pirate Boat, V&A Waterfront, 021 421 0909. SUP Cape Town, Dock Road, V&A Waterfront, 082 789 0411. Scratch Patch/Cave Golf, Dock Road, V&A Waterfront, 021 419 9429.
Eat: Willoughby and Co., V&A Waterfront Shopping Centre, 021 418 6115. Cape Town Fish Market, V&A Waterfront Clock Tower, 021 418 5977. Grand Café and Beach, Haul Road, Granger Bay, 021 425 0551.
Shop: Toy Kingdom, V&A Waterfront Shopping Centre, 021 421 1192. Peggity's Toys, V&A Waterfront Shopping Centre, 021 419 6873. Cape Union Mart, V&A Waterfront Shopping Centre, 021 419 0019.
Sleep: The Table Bay Hotel, V&A Waterfront, 021 406 5000. One&Only Cape Town, Dock Road, V&A Waterfront, 021 431 5888.
For parents: Cape Town Comedy Club (formerly Jou Ma Se Comedy Club), Dock Road, V&A Waterfront, 021 418 8880.

Special event
Galileo open-air cinema on the croquet lawn seasonally

23 Zip Zap Circus shows
www.zip-zap.co.za

A highly regarded, active social circus and innovative school of circus arts, made up of children from seven years old, performs shows for the public throughout the year. It has been affiliated with Cirque du Soleil. Much of their focus now is on performing in fundraising shows for various NPOs. Children will be thrilled at Zip Zap's circus acts, which include an entertaining manipulation of the yo-yo, a solo act on a single rope, an audience interactive comedy act, hilarious antics combining slapstick and acrobatics, the spinning Cyr wheel act, contortion, and a highly choreographed trapeze act.

Tel number	021 421 8622
Address	Founders Garden, Jan Smuts Street, Foreshore
GPS marker	33°55'09"S; 18°25'52"E
Closest public transport	MyCiTi bus route 101
Opening hours	Depends on show time
Most appropriate age group	6+
Pram/wheelchair-friendly	Yes, and people in wheelchairs can use the Artscape toilets across the road
Baby-changing facility	Yes, there is a table to use
Nearest hospital	Netcare Christiaan Barnard Memorial Hospital, 021 480 6111

COST R50 to R70

Cape Town: Southern Suburbs

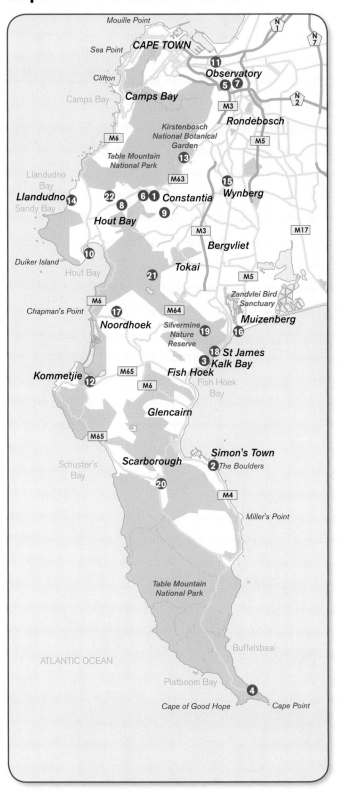

1. Acrobranch
2. Boulders Beach and Penguin Colony
3. Brass Bell
4. Cape Point Nature Reserve
5. Cape Town Science Centre
6. Cape Town Zipline Tour
7. City Rock Indoor Climbing
8. Clay Café
9. Constantia Greenbelt
10. Duiker Island boat trip
11. Hint Hunt
12. Imhoff Farm
13. Kirstenbosch National Botanical Garden
14. Llandudno Beach
15. Maynardville Park and Open-air Theatre
16. Muizenberg Water Slides
17. Noordhoek Farm Village
18. St James Beach
19. Silvermine Nature Reserve
20. SunScene Outdoor Adventure Course
21. Tokai Forest
22. World of Birds Wildlife Sanctuary and Monkey Park

1 Acrobranch
www.acrobranch.co.za

5/5
Party venue rating

0/5
Rainy day option

For two hours, you and your child can swing through the trees on one of three action-packed aerial courses. Each one is designed to offer all members of the family an exhilarating, challenging outdoor experience through the forest, with routes designed specifically for children and a course for reasonably fit adults and teenagers. Obstacles consist of zip lines, tree-top high ropes and tricky crossings by ladder, tunnel, walkway and bridge. Children are fitted snugly into harnesses and hooked into secure lines all through the course, and they are closely supervised. The children are, however, encouraged to move their own clips to get the full experience.

Tel number	021 201 1121 or 086 999 0369
Address	1 Hout Bay Road, Hout Bay
GPS marker	34°00'44"S; 18°24'19"E
Closest public transport	MyCiTi bus route 108 or 109
Opening hours	9am–5pm Tuesday to Sunday and public holidays
Most appropriate age group	7+
Pram/wheelchair-friendly	Yes
Baby-changing facility	No
Nearest hospital	Mediclinic Constantiaberg, 021 799 2911

Take note: There is an Acrobranch in Wilderness if you're road tripping along the Garden Route.

COST R100 or R140 or R180

② Boulders Beach and Penguin Colony
www.tmnp.co.za

3/5 Party venue rating

2/5 Rainy day option

Glencairn

Simon's Town
② The Boulders

borough

20

M4

Miller's Point

Bay

This beach is ideal for children as large boulders shelter the cove from big, rough waves, offering a warm ocean swimming experience. It is home to a breeding colony of over 2,000 endangered African penguins and forms part of the Table Mountain National Park Marine Protected Area. Explore the large, ancient granite boulders, small rock pools and little bays with your child and get close to the African penguins and their nesting and breeding sites via a walkway. For picnics on the beach, you're encouraged to get to the beach at low tide as the amount of space on the sand depends on the tides.

Tel number	021 786 2329
Address	Kleintuin Road, Simon's Town
GPS marker	34°11'53"S; 18°27'12"E
Closest public transport	Simon's Town Railway Station, Metrorail
Opening hours	7am–7:30pm December to January, 8am–6:30pm February to April, 8am–5pm May to September, 8am–6:30pm October to November
Most appropriate age group	6+
Pram/wheelchair-friendly	Yes
Baby-changing facility	Yes
Nearest hospital	False Bay Hospital, 021 782 1121

Nearby
Visit/see: Just Nuisance community market (usually once a month), Jubilee Square in summer and Simon's Town City Hall in winter, 082 088 7174. The SA Naval Museum, St George's Street, 021 786 5243.
Play/do: Scratch Patch, Dido Valley Road, Simon's Town, 021 786 2020.
Eat: Boulders Beach Restaurant, Boulders Beach Lodge, Boulders Place, Simon's Town, 021 786 1758. Lekker, St George's Street, Simon's Town, 021 786 1163. Bertha's, Wharf Street, Simon's Town, 021 786 2138. The Meeting Place, St George's Street, Simon's Town, 021 786 5678. Baracuda's, corner Beach and Recreation roads, Fish Hoek, 021 782 3066. Black Marlin, Miller's Point, Simon's Town, 021 786 1621. Seaforth Restaurant, Seaforth Beach, Seaforth Road, Simon's Town, 021 786 4810.

COST

R30 for children 2–11 years old and R60 for adults

Special event
Simon's Town Navy Festival

③ Brass Bell
www.brassbell.co.za

 3/5 Party venue rating

 5/5 Rainy day option

Sit at eye level with the ocean and enjoy unpretentious, quality seafood, regular live entertainment and the energy that this restaurant draws from the bustling, arty fishing village of Kalk Bay. There are many venues within the Brass Bell, offering different dining experiences, and families are welcome at most of them. Those to earmark are the alfresco options, namely the Water's Edge Terrace, with seating that goes right onto the edge of the tidal pool (you're so close to the water that the waves sometimes wash up into the venue) and The Beach at The Bell, which has a paddling pool for little ones.

Tel number	021 788 5455
Address	Kalk Bay Station, Main Road, Kalk Bay
GPS marker	34°07'34"S; 18°27'01"E
Closest public transport	Kalk Bay Railway Station
Opening hours	8am or 9am till late daily
Most appropriate age group	6+
Pram/wheelchair-friendly	No
Baby-changing facility	Yes
Nearest hospital	False Bay Hospital, 021 782 1121

Nearby
<u>Visit/see</u>: Kalk Bay Theatre, Main Road, 021 788 7257. The Kalk Bay Harbour.
<u>Play/do</u>: Kalk Bay Park and Bob's Bagel Café, Rouxville Road, Kalk Bay, 083 280 0012.
<u>Eat</u>: The Ice Café, Main Road, Kalk Bay, 021 788 4816.
<u>Shop</u>: Kalk Bay Co-op, Main Road, Kalk Bay. Kalk Bay Books, Main Road, 021 788 2266, and numerous vintage and antique shops.

④ Cape Point Nature Reserve
www.capepoint.co.za

 **3/5** Party venue rating

 2/5 Rainy day option

Children will love riding the Flying Dutchman Funicular up to the renowned viewing point on the reserve, below the old lighthouse. On a hot day, enjoy the great swimming spots, picnic sites and walks in and around the tidal pools. Walk the shipwreck trail to view a few of the 26 recorded shipwrecks. The Two Oceans Restaurant is inside the reserve and boasts a wooden deck that looks out onto one of the most breathtaking ocean views in the country.

Take note: South Africans qualify for a My Green Card for discounted entrance into the reserve.

Tel number	021 780 9010
Address	Cape Point Road
GPS marker	34°15'41"S; 18°27'29"E
Closest public transport	Simon's Town Railway Station, Metrorail or The Green Bus
Opening hours	6am–6pm October to March, 7am–5pm April to September
Most appropriate age group	2+
Pram/wheelchair-friendly	Yes
Baby-changing facility	Yes
Nearest hospital	False Bay Hospital, 021 782 1121

Nearby
Eat: Cape Point Vineyards, Silvermine Road, Noord-hoek, 021 789 0900 (a pit stop on your way to or from Cape Point Nature Reserve).

Special event
SANParks Week

COST
R55 per child and
R110 per adult

---

5 **Cape Town Science Centre**
www.ctsc.org.za

The centre offers more than 250 interactive exhibits and puzzles, displays, science shows, curriculum-based workshops, science camps, science theatre, travelling exhibitions, hands-on experiments, excursions, Saturday learner enrichment school, robotics workshops and tournaments, and chess workshops and tournaments. Be sure to enquire about their school holiday programmes, which are open to everyone of schoolgoing age and include various workshops, shows and activities. For about R5 a week, Science Centre members enjoy unlimited visits to the centre for one year, plus access to special members-only events.

COST
R45 for 3–18-year-olds and adults, R25 for pensioners and students

Tel number	021 300 3200
Address	Main Road, Observatory
GPS marker	33°56'18"S; 18°27'51"E
Closest public transport	Observatory Railway Station, Metrorail
Opening hours	9am–4:30pm Monday to Saturday, 10am–4:30pm Sunday
Most appropriate age group	3+
Pram/wheelchair-friendly	Yes, via the entrance at the back gate
Baby-changing facility	Yes
Nearest hospital	Groote Schuur Hospital, 021 404 9111

Nearby

<u>Visit/see</u>: South African Astronomical Observatory, Observatory Road, Observatory, 021 447 0025.
<u>Play/do</u>: Rococoa Chocolate Factory, Palms Centre, Sir Lowry Road, Woodstock, 021 461 2301. The Playshed, Oude Molen Eco Village, Alexandra Road, Pinelands, 021 801 0141/2.
<u>Eat</u>: The River Club, corner Liesbeek Parkway and Observatory Road, Observatory, 021 448 6117. Millstone Farmstall and Café, Oude Molen Eco Village, Alexandra Road, Pinelands, 021 447 8226.

Special event

Science Out Loud Popular Science Talks

6 Cape Town Zipline Tour
www.saforestadventures.co.za

This exhilarating aerial cable slide, located on the private Silvermist Wine Estate, is based on the popular zip-line tours in Hermanus, Caledon and Citrusdal. The cables are up to 500m long and up to 155m above the tree canopy. After registration, a safety briefing and demonstration by your guides at the base camp, you will travel by 4x4 high into the mountain for 2km. Once the guides have ensured your comfort, the fun can begin and you will be gliding and zip lining in between the canyons with the tree canopy far below your feet. Some platforms and zip lines, as they climb higher, will test you. The estate has a restaurant where you can gather the family to refuel and share stories from the day.

Take note:
You are strongly advised to think twice before booking if you have a fear of heights. Make sure your child is really up for it.

Tel number	083 517 3635
Address	Silvermist Private Estate, Hout Bay Road, Constantia Nek
GPS marker	34°00'44"S; 18°24'09"E
Closest public transport	City Sightseeing bus blue route
Opening hours	9am–5:30pm in summer or until 3:30pm in winter
Most appropriate age group	8+
Pram/wheelchair-friendly	No
Baby-changing facility	No
Nearest hospital	Mediclinic Constantiaberg, 021 799 2911

COST From R480 per person

---

7 **City Rock Indoor Climbing**
www.cityrock.co.za

5/5
Party venue rating

5/5
Rainy day option

Something a little daring but safe, this climbing gym will allow your whole family to get involved. There are three climbing options for children: bouldering is the easiest and least expensive as the climbing is not high and does not require a rope. The automatic belay wall is an introduction to high climbing – the rope is attached to a braking system at the top of the wall and will lower your child gently back down to the ground, if necessary. High-wall top roping enables the child to climb if he has someone to do the necessary rope work for belaying (arrest a fall) – one of the child's parents can do it if they have the certification.

Tel number	021 447 1326
Address	Anson Street, Observatory
GPS marker	33°56'12"S; 18°28'14"E
Closest public transport	Observatory Railway Station, Metrorail
Opening hours	9am–9pm Monday and Wednesday, 9am–10pm Tuesday and Thursday, 9am–6pm Friday to Sunday, 10am–6pm public holidays
Most appropriate age group	6+
Pram/wheelchair-friendly	No
Baby-changing facility	Yes
Nearest hospital	Groote Schuur Hospital, 021 404 9111

COST From R80 per child and R100 per adult

---

8 Clay Café
www.claycafe.co.za

 5/5 Party venue rating

 5/5 Rainy day option

A supreme family venue that offers ceramic bisque blanks for children to paint and a place for parents to sit back and relax. Children choose from an array of unfired bisque and a wide selection of colourful paints to create crockery. The Clay Café does the glazing and firing. There is also a children's playground, a bouncy net and a skateboard half-pipe ramp especially for children under 14 years old. They are open till late on Thursdays for pizza night, painting and playing.

Tel number	021 790 3318
Address	Old Oakhurst Dairy Farm, Main Road, Hout Bay
GPS marker	34°01'07"S; 18°22'38"E
Closest public transport	MyCiTi bus route 109
Opening hours	9am–5pm daily and on Thursday 9am–9pm
Most appropriate age group	5+
Pram/wheelchair-friendly	Yes
Baby-changing facility	No
Nearest hospital	Hout Bay Medical Centre, 021 790 3120

9 Constantia Greenbelt

www.zandvleitrust.org.za

 0/5 Party venue rating

 1/5 Rainy day option

The Constantia Valley Greenbelt comprises nine easy interlinking walking trails each 30–45 minutes long. Children will love exploring the green paths and streams and getting that enchanted forest feeling. Dogs are welcome. The Zandvlei Trust website has maps of each route.

Address	Constantia Valley
GPS marker	34°01'30"S; 18°26'01"E
Closest public transport	City Sightseeing bus blue route
Most appropriate age group	4+
Pram/wheelchair-friendly	No
Baby-changing facility	No
Nearest hospital	Mediclinic Constantiaberg, 021 799 2911

Nearby

Eat: Constantia Nek Restaurant, Hout Bay Road, Constantia, 021 794 5132. River Café, Spaanschemat River Road, Constantia, 021 794 3010. Simon's at Groot Constantia (also great for picnics), 021 794 1143. The Clubhouse at Claremont Cricket Club, Constantia Sports Complex, 021 794 6314.

Shop: Constantia Village, corner Constantia Main and Spaanschemat River roads, Constantia, 021 794 5065.

For parents: Alphen Hotel, Alphen Drive, 021 795 6300.

Special events

The Grape Run
The Teddy Bear Fair

---

10 Duiker Island boat trip

www.drumbeatcharters.co.za

 4/5 Party venue rating

 4/5 Rainy day option

Enjoy a boat trip from Hout Bay Harbour to Duiker Island (Seal Island), home to thousands of Cape fur seals. Drumbeat Charters has been operating cruises on purpose-designed vessels for the past 20 years, which afford your child the excitement of getting really close to wildlife in their natural habitat.

Tel number	021 791 4441 or 082 658 7055
Address	Hout Bay Harbour
GPS marker	34°02'57"S; 18°20'49"E
Closest public transport	MyCiTi bus route 109
Opening hours	From 8:30am
Most appropriate age group	4+
Pram/wheelchair-friendly	Yes
Baby-changing facility	Yes, although please take a mat
Nearest hospital	Hout Bay Medical Centre, 021 790 3120

Nearby

Visit/see: Bay Harbour Market, Harbour Road, Hout Bay. Mariner's Wharf, Hout Bay Harbour, 021 790 1100. Hout Bay Museum, Andrews Road, 021 790 3270.
Play/do: Valley Farmstall, Valley Road, 021 790 3803. Hout Bay Beach.
Eat: Chapman's Peak Hotel, Chapman's Peak Drive, Hout Bay, 021 790 1036. Ragafellows, Main Road, Scott Estate, 021 790 8955. Dune's, Beach Crescent, Scott Estate, 021 790 1876. Snoekie's, Quay 4, Harbour Road, Hout Bay, 021 790 6677. Spiro's, Main Road, Hout Bay, 021 791 3897. Quentin at Oakhurst, Dorman Way, Hout Bay, 021 790 4888.
Sleep: Hout Bay Manor, Baviaanskloof Road, Scott Estate, 021 790 0116.

---

11 Hint Hunt
www.hinthunt.co.za

5/5 Party venue rating

5/5 Rainy day option

This is a fast-paced, brain-twisting escape game that was first discovered in London and brought to Cape Town in 2013. In this challenge, your family of three, four, five or six is locked up in a small room for a bout of pretend detective play. You have to solve riddles, decode puzzles and navigate a mountain of mysteries in order to get out of the space before the 60-minute time limit is up. There are two different types of rooms you can opt for – the complex zen room or the slightly easier John Monroe's office. The rooms are indoors, making the game perfect for windy and rainy days. Great for families with older children.

COST R130–R195 per person

Tel number	021 448 9864
Address	The Old Biscuit Mill, Woodstock
GPS marker	33°55'40"S; 18°27'28"E
Closest public transport	Woodstock Railway Station, Metrorail or MyCiTi bus route 102
Opening hours	Slots available 1:30pm–8:15pm Monday to Thursday, 9:45am–8:15pm Friday and Saturday, 10am–4pm Sunday
Most appropriate age group	9+
Pram/wheelchair-friendly	Yes
Baby-changing facility	Yes
Nearest hospital	Groote Schuur Hospital, 021 404 9111
	Life Vincent Pallotti Hospital, 021 506 5111

Nearby

Visit/see: The Neighbourgoods Market, The Old Biscuit Mill, Woodstock.
Play/do: The Woodstock Foundry, 170 Albert Road, Woodstock, 021 422 0466.
Eat: The Kitchen, Sir Lowry Road, Woodstock, 021 462 2201.
Shop: Woodstock Exchange, 66 Albert Road, 021 486 5999.
For parents: A Luke Dale-Roberts eatery in The Old Biscuit Mill: Pot Luck Club, 021 447 0804, or The Test Kitchen, 021 447 2337.

---

12 Imhoff Farm
www.imhofffarm.co.za

 5/5 Party venue rating

 4/5 Rainy day option

This Cape farmstead, a little Cape Town enclave for families, offers all things country, from stunning views to organic produce. Of particular interest to parents is all the entertainment they offer children – camel rides, cart rides, face painting, the Higgeldy Piggeldy Farmyard, horse riding, paintball and a snake park, which runs an interesting presentation every Sunday afternoon, as well as a mobile show for birthday parties called the Minni Mo Reptile Show. Situated next to the farmyard and with a dedicated children's menu, an enclosed garden and jungle gym, the Blue Water Café is a fantastic spot to take the family.

Tel number	021 783 4545
Address	Kommetjie Road, Kommetjie
GPS marker	34°08'35"S; 18°21'06"E
Closest public transport	Fish Hoek Railway Station, Metrorail
Opening hours	8am/9am–5pm
Most appropriate age group	3+
Pram/wheelchair-friendly	Yes
Baby-changing facility	Yes
Nearest hospital	False Bay Hospital, 021 782 1121

Nearby

Visit/see: Slangkop Lighthouse, Lighthouse Road, Kommetjie, 021 783 1717. Harry Goeman's Garden Centre, Kommetjie Road, 021 785 3201.
Play/do: Zizamele Ceramics, Imhoff Farm, Kommetjie Road, 021 789 1491.

⑬ Kirstenbosch National Botanical Garden
www.sanbi.org

Along with nature explorations and picnics, this World Heritage Site offers the Boomslang, which is a tree canopy walkway designed to provide aerial views of the garden, and Moyo for fun, child-friendly dining and South African cuisine. Every summer season sees the return of the Summer Sunset Concerts on Sundays along with the Galileo open-air cinema nights. The Gold Fields Environmental Educational Centre engages schoolgoing children in biodiversity, conservation and environmental education. During the holidays the centre usually runs the Nature's Treasure Box art workshop for young children, which involves collecting some of nature's treasures while on a walk through the garden.

Tel number	021 799 8783
Address	Rhodes Drive, Newlands
GPS marker	33°59'17"S; 18°26'08"E
Closest public transport	Claremont Railway Station, Metrorail
Opening hours	8am–7pm September to March, 8am–6pm April to August
Most appropriate age group	6+
Pram/wheelchair-friendly	Yes
Baby-changing facility	Yes
Nearest hospital	Life Claremont Hospital, 021 670 4300

Nearby
Visit/see: Newlands Cricket Ground, Campground Road, Newlands, 021 657 2050.
Play/do: Newlands Forest, 021 422 1601/2. Rush Indoor Trampoline Park, Stadium-on-Main, Claremont, 082 460 5388. My Space to Create, Newlands, 072 250 0045. Kenilworth Karting, Myhof Road, Claremont, 021 683 2670.
Shop: Cavendish, Dreyer Street, Claremont, 021 657 5620. The Fairy Shop, Palmyra Road, Claremont, 021 671 0935.
For parents: Newlands Brewery Tour, Main Road, Newlands, 021 658 7440/448.

COST: R10 for 6–17-year-olds and R50 per adult

14 Llandudno Beach
www.capetown.gov.za

 3/5 Party venue rating

 0/5 Rainy day option

Llandudno is a coastal residential area that famously has no shops or streetlights. Its wind-protected Blue Flag beach, surrounded by large granite boulders and a mountainous backdrop, is the locals' favourite. It is one of Cape Town's most picturesque beaches, hugely popular among surfers and a fantastic location for a sunset picnic.

Address	Victoria Road, Llandudno
GPS marker	34°00'30"S; 18°20'32"E
Closest public transport	MyCiTi bus route 109
Most appropriate age group	5+
Pram/wheelchair-friendly	No
Baby-changing facility	No
Nearest hospital	Hout Bay Medical Centre, 021 790 3120

Nearby
Eat: High tea at The Twelve Apostles Hotel's Conservatory, Victoria Road, Camps Bay, 021 437 9029.

15 Maynardville Park and Open-air Theatre

 4/5 Party venue rating

 1/5 Rainy day option

This southern suburbs park offers rolling lawns and trees, and a well-equipped children's playground. One of the charms of the park is the Krakeelwater Pond, which is brought to life by its own busy network of birds. The park also has a dedicated open-air theatre, which was established in the mid-1950s. It characteristically hosts classical theatre and dance, with the annual Shakespeare in the Park productions being a huge focus as they usually tackle the matric set work for the year at government schools. This venue has much to offer a family – from a picnic beneath the stars, watching a play, cycling and walking your dog to attending one of the park's carnivals, fairs, markets and motor shows.

Tel number	021 444 8849
Address	Corner Church and Wolfe streets, Wynberg
GPS marker	34°00'16"S; 18°27'49"E
Closest public transport	Wynberg Railway Station, Metrorail
Opening hours	7am–7pm September to March, 7:30am–6pm April to August
Most appropriate age group	1+
Pram/wheelchair-friendly	Yes
Baby-changing facility	No
Nearest hospital	Life Kingsbury Hospital, 021 670 4000

Nearby

Visit/see: Chart Farm, Klaassens Road, Wynberg Park, 021 761 0434. Baxter Theatre, Rondebosch, 021 685 7880.
Play/do: College of Magic, Imam Haron Road, 021 683 0988.
Eat: Four and Twenty, Wolfe Street, Wynberg, 021 762 0975.

Special events

Community Chest Carnival and Stellenberg Open Gardens

16 Muizenberg Water Slides

www.muizenbergslides.co.za

Situated next to Muizenberg Beach, this outdoor venue offers three water slides – one advanced slide, one straight-and-fast speed slide and one junior slide for smaller children. The pools are solar heated and there is shaded seating and tables for picnics. There is a tuck shop on site where you can buy refreshments – chips and sweets as well as hotdogs and hot drinks. The slides are open from mid-September to April with extended hours during the holidays, so you should quite literally strike while it's hot. There are bathrooms on site and parking is available outside the venue.

COST R80 for a full-day pass

Tel number	021 788 4759 or 082 454 5023
Address	Beach Road, Muizenberg
GPS marker	34°06'19"S; 18°28'30"E
Closest public transport	Muizenberg Railway Station, Metrorail
Opening hours	1:30pm–5:30pm Monday to Friday, 6pm–9pm Friday, 9:30am–5:30pm Saturday and Sunday during the school term, and 9:30am–5:30pm Monday to Sunday, 6pm–9pm Friday during school holidays; open mid-September to April
Most appropriate age group	3+
Pram/wheelchair-friendly	Yes
Baby-changing facility	No
Nearest hospital	False Bay Hospital, 021 782 1121 or Mediclinic Constantiaberg, 021 799 2911

Nearby

Visit/see: Bluebird Garage Market, Albertyn Road, Muizenberg.

Play/do: Planet Kids, Wherry Road, Muizenberg, 021 788 3070. Surf at Muizenberg Beach; use Roxy's Surf School, 021 788 8687, Gary's Surf School, 021 788 9839 or Learn to Surf, 083 414 0567.

Eat: Tiger's Milk, Surfers' Corner, Beach Road, Muizenberg, 021 788 1869/1860. Knead Bakery, Surfers' Corner, Beach Road, Muizenberg, 021 788 2909. Lucky Fish and Chips, Beach Road, Muizenberg, 021 788 9597. Primi Piatti, Surfers' Corner, Beach Road, Muizenberg, 021 788 7130.

Shop: The Corner Surf Shop, Main Road, Marina Da Gama, Muizenberg, 021 788 1191.

---

(17) Noordhoek Farm Village

www.noordhoekvillage.co.za

5/5 Party venue rating

4/5 Rainy day option

The Village offers a safe and welcoming environment for you to shop, eat and play. The playground has been designed to accommodate various age groups – the high-activity zones for older children are physically separated from the low-activity zones for children of younger ages. These play areas are visible from any location in the playground and from Café Roux. All four of the village's restaurants are child-friendly and the various shops cater for children, selling sweets and toys, children's and baby wear, African storybooks, fluffy toys and tie-dyed T-shirts.

Address	Village Lane and Noordhoek Main Road, Noordhoek
GPS marker	34°05'48"S; 18°22'38"E
Closest public transport	Fish Hoek Railway Station
Opening hours	9am–5pm daily
Most appropriate age group	1+
Pram/wheelchair-friendly	Yes
Baby-changing facility	Yes
Nearest hospital	False Bay Hospital, 021 782 1121
	Mediclinic Constantiaberg, 021 799 2911

18 St James Beach

 5/5 Party venue rating
 2/5 Rainy day option

St James offers an intimate beach, a large tidal pool and rock pools along the False Bay coastline. Its colourful beach huts are a trademark. This beach holds particular appeal for children as the tidal pool is calmer and warmer than the sea, which makes for pleasant bathing conditions. When you're not enjoying a swim, take a stroll along the pathway that links St James with Surfers' Corner in Muizenberg. You are allowed to lock your valuables in one of the iconic colourful huts, so the whole family can frolic in the water together.

Address	Main Road, St James
GPS marker	34°07'08"S; 18°27'33"E
Closest public transport	St James Railway Station, Metrorail
Most appropriate age group	4+
Pram/wheelchair-friendly	Yes
Baby-changing facility	No
Nearest hospital	False Bay Hospital, 021 782 1121

Nearby
Visit/see: Save Our Seas Shark Centre, Main Road, Kalk Bay, 021 788 6694.
Play/do: Old Mule Contour Path, Boyes Drive, above St James.
Eat: The Octopus Garden, The Old Post Office Building, Main Road, St James, 021 788 5646.

19 Silvermine Nature Reserve
www.tmnp.co.za

 5/5 Party venue rating **2/5** Rainy day option

With a reservoir you can swim in and several designated spots around the reservoir to braai (not in summer) or picnic, this iconic Cape Town venue is one of the best spots to gather family and friends to make the most of clear days. There is a boardwalk accessible to prams, and many walks to enjoy. Remember to pack everyone's bikes and cash for permits to tackle any of the MTB trails. You can take your dogs, too, but the annual permit only allows access to the far side of the reservoir.

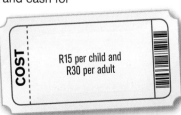

COST: R15 per child and R30 per adult

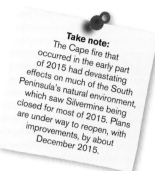

Take note:
The Cape fire that occurred in the early part of 2015 had devastating effects on much of the South Peninsula's natural environment, which saw Silvermine being closed for most of 2015. Plans are under way to reopen, with improvements, by about December 2015.

Address	Silvermine Homestead, Ou Kaapseweg, Noordhoek
GPS marker	34°05'13"S; 18°25'28"E
Closest public transport	Fish Hoek Railway Station, Metrorail
Opening hours	8am–5pm October to April,
	7am–6pm May to September
Most appropriate age group	1+
Pram/wheelchair-friendly	Yes
Baby-changing facility	Yes
Nearest hospital	False Bay Hospital, 021 782 1121
	Mediclinic Constantiaberg, 021 799 2911

Nearby

Visit/see: Noordhoek Common, Avondrust Circle.

Play/do: Long Beach, 1 Kirsten Avenue, Kommetjie. Chapman's Peak Drive (the preferred route to Noordhoek), 021 791 8222.

Eat: Thorfynn's Restaurant, Monkey Valley Resort, Mountain Road, Chapman's Peak, 021 789 8000. The Foodbarn, Noordhoek Farm Village, Village Lane, 021 789 1390.

Special event

Park Run

---

20 # SunScene Outdoor Adventure Course
www.sunscene.co.za

This specially built course offers a variety of challenging activities for large groups of children to tackle, such as uneven posts, angled balance beams, swinging logs, a wonky bridge, paintball target shooting, live wire, spider's web, vertical assault wall, climbing tree and a 130m zip slide. The team of expert guides also offers surfing and sandboarding.

Tel number	021 783 0203
Address	Cape Farmhouse, junction of Redhill and Plateau roads, Scarborough
GPS marker	34°12'20"S; 18°24'23"E
Closest public transport	Simon's Town Railway Station, Metrorail
Opening hours	Call to book and for costs
Most appropriate age group	6+
Pram/wheelchair-friendly	Yes
Baby-changing facility	No
Nearest hospital	False Bay Hospital, 021 782 1121

Nearby

Visit/see: Schusterskraal Beach, Scarborough.
Eat: Cape Farmhouse, junction of Redhill and Plateau roads, 021 780 1246.

21 Tokai Forest

www.tmnp.co.za

5/5
Party venue rating

1/5
Rainy day option

The forest is a firm favourite for hiking, horse riding, dog walking, cycling, braais and picnics. The forest's shady arboretum forms the base of most hikes, with the 6km hike up to Elephant's Eye Cave being one of the most popular. The shady braai and picnic spots are spacious and offer ample space to spend a peaceful afternoon while the children run around playing hide-and-seek.

Take note:
After the damaging Cape fire that occurred in the first half of 2015, the Tokai forest area has had to be closed. It will re-open in phases as areas are declared safe after the fire.

Address	Tokai Road, Tokai
GPS marker	34°03'41"S; 18°24'54"E
Closest public transport	Retreat Railway Station, Metrorail
Opening hours	7am–6pm October to March, 8am–5pm April to September
Most appropriate age group	1+
Pram/wheelchair-friendly	Yes
Baby-changing facility	No
Nearest hospital	Medicross Tokai, 021 710 9950

Nearby
Visit/see: Tokai Forest Market, Tokai Road, 072 538 8793.
Eat: Lister's Place, Tokai Arboretum, 021 715 4512.
Shop: Earth Fair Market, Main Street, Retreat. Reader's
Warehouse, corner Bark and Main roads, 021 701 0632.

COST R20 per adult, R10 per child, R15 per car

 World of Birds Wildlife Sanctuary and Monkey Park
www.worldofbirds.org.za

5/5 Party venue rating
3/5 Rainy day option

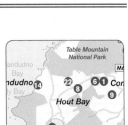

A tropical garden in the Hout Bay valley is home to Africa's largest bird park, with over 3,000 birds and small animals of 400 different species presented in more than 100 spacious walk-through aviaries. The Monkey Jungle, with its cute squirrel monkeys, is a real highlight for the children. To help you explore with busy children, World of Birds rents out children's pushcarts, and there is a playground for them too. The Robin's Nest offers drinks, snacks and light meals, or you can have a picnic on the Flamingo Terrace, right next to the flamingos.

Take note:
In preparation for this day out, print the helpful World of Birds map to be found on their website.

Tel number	021 790 2730
Address	Valley Road, Hout Bay
GPS marker	34°01'04"S; 18°21'46"E
Closest public transport	MyCiTi bus route 109
Opening hours	9am–5pm daily
Most appropriate age group	3+
Pram/wheelchair-friendly	No
Baby-changing facility	Yes
Nearest hospital	Hout Bay Medical Centre, 021 790 3120

COST Adults R85, children R40, pensioners R55

Cape Town: Northern Suburbs

1. Blasters
2. Blouberg Beach
3. Bugz Family Playpark
4. GrandWest Casino and Entertainment World
5. Intaka Island
6. Ratanga Junction Theme Park
7. The White House Stables outrides

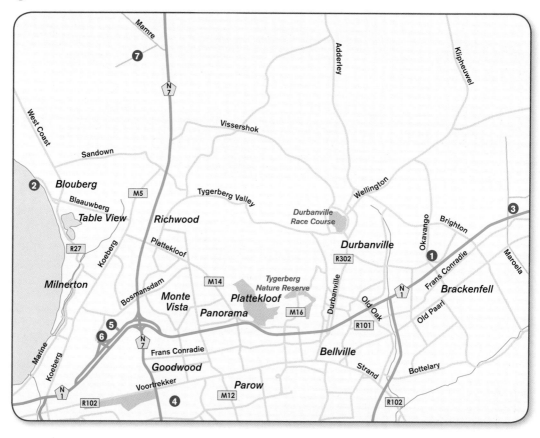

1 Blasters
www.blasters.co.za

5/5 Party venue rating

5/5 Rainy day option

You can enjoy breakfast, lunch, dinner or coffee while the children play, or you can drop your child off for a few hours while you do your shopping as Blasters has high-tech electronic tagging to ensure each child's safety and security. The indoor play area is supervised by trained attendants, is one of the largest play spaces in Cape Town within a restaurant setting, and is cleaned and disinfected daily. There are two separate play areas to accommodate specific age groups, namely a soft play area for 0–3-year-olds and a play area dedicated to children 4–12 years old.

Tel number	021 981 7555
Address	CapeGate Décor Centre, shop A1, Nitida Avenue, Kleinbron Park, Brackenfell
GPS marker	33°51'00"S; 18°41'41"E
Closest public transport	Brackenfell Railway Station, Metrorail
Opening hours	9am–10pm Monday to Saturday, 9am–6pm Sunday
Most appropriate age group	1–12
Pram/wheelchair-friendly	Yes; for wheelchair access be sure to park in the undercover parking area
Baby-changing facility	Yes
Nearest hospital	Mediclinic CapeGate, 021 983 5600

COST: Adults free, children 4 years and older R40, children under 4 years old R30

---

② Blouberg Beach

 3/5 Party venue rating   0/5 Rainy day option

A long stretch of sandy white beach that is a hotspot for the exciting spectator sport of kite surfing. Big Bay is popular for families of older children as they can surf under lifeguard presence. A gem for families with small children in the Blouberg region is Small Bay. The beach is protected from the wind and the water is calm, which means surfers stay away, making it safe for the children to swim. There is a park on a grassed area just off the beach with a large jungle gym. Small Bay buzzes with family activities, especially at sunset.

GPS marker	33°47'44"S; 18°27'27"E
Closest public transport	MyCiTi bus route 217
Most appropriate age group	2+
Pram/wheelchair-friendly	Yes
Baby-changing facility	No
Nearest hospital	Netcare Blaauwberg Hospital, 021 554 9000

Nearby
Play/do: Atlantis Dunes sandboarding, Sidewinder Sandboarding Adventures, Oviston Road, Edgemead, 072 177 8620.
Shop: Eden on the Bay Mall, corner Otto du Plessis and Sir David Baird drives, Bloubergstrand, 021 554 9700.

(3) Bugz Family Playpark
www.bugzplaypark.co.za

5/5
Party venue rating

4/5
Rainy day option

Bugz is the largest playpark in the Western Cape, with an outdoor playground and indoor play area. There is place for freeplay – Bugz has two large sandpit areas with jungle gyms, slides, swings and various play equipment to crawl under or climb over. Magic shows take place most Saturdays and Sundays. The token rides available on weekends, public and school holidays are numerous and include the choo-choo train, quad bikes and the swing horse as well as something for the younger age group, the toddler tractor. Children can also engage with the roaming, resident Bugz characters. The Bugz Tent Kitchen makes a tasty selection of food for both adults and children.

Tel number	021 988 8836
Address	56 Tarentaal Street, Kraaifontein
GPS marker	33°49'58"S; 18°44'15"E
Closest public transport	Kraaifontein Railway Station, Metrorail
Opening hours	9am–5pm daily
Most appropriate age group	3–10
Pram/wheelchair-friendly	Yes
Baby-changing facility	Yes
Nearest hospital	Mediclinic Durbanville, 021 980 2100

Nearby
Visit/see: Bellville Library, Carl van Aswegen Street, Bellville, 021 444 0300.
Shop: Plasticland, Carl Cronjé Street, Tygervalley, 021 914 5700.

COST
R35–R45 per child and R5 per token ride, R35 per adult

Take note:
The VIP card gets you access to the play-park and unlimited rides, usually for a year, but sometimes the Bugz are really generous and make the VIP card valid for longer.

4 GrandWest Casino and Entertainment World
www.suninternational.com/grandwest

The indoor family-friendly activities at this casino complex are plentiful, so it's ideal for winter days. There is ice skating – the Ice Station boasts an Olympic-sized skating rink and a mini supervised rink for children under five years old and no taller than 1.3m. There is a 12-lane tenpin bowling area with music for added atmosphere, and the Kids' Corner Crèche is a supervised fun environment for children up to 10 years old. The Magic Arcade is for traditional arcade games, and there are movie cinemas.

Tel number	021 505 7777
Address	1 Jakes Gerwel Drive, Goodwood
GPS marker	33°55'07"S; 18°32'41"E
Closest public transport	Goodwood Railway Station, Metrorail
Opening hours	Vary per venue
Most appropriate age group	3+
Pram/wheelchair-friendly	Yes
Baby-changing facility	Yes
Nearest hospital	Netcare N1 City Hosptial, 021 590 4444

Nearby
Shop: N1 City Mall, Louwtjie Rothman Street, Goodwood, 021 595 1170.

COST — A nominal parking fee for entry applies

5 Intaka Island
www.intaka.co.za

Take your family to this peaceful wetland and bird sanctuary. Apart from the walks to be enjoyed, take the family on a 35-minute ferry ride on the Grand Canal and around the island. There is a special hop-on, hop-off feature at Canal Walk and Crystal Towers Hotel during school holidays.

COST — R8.50 for under 12s, R14 per adult

Tel number	021 552 6889
Address	Park Way, Century City
GPS marker	33°53'18"S; 18°30'49"E
Closest public transport	Century City Railway Station, Metrorail and MyCiTi bus route 251
Opening hours	7:30am–5:30pm May to September, 7:30am–7pm October to April
Most appropriate age group	5+
Pram/wheelchair-friendly	Yes
Baby-changing facility	No
Nearest hospital	Canal Walk Medical Centre, 021 552 8080 Netcare N1 City Hospital, 021 590 4444

Nearby

<u>Visit/see</u>: China Town, Sable Square, Milnerton, 071 238 1558.

<u>Play/do</u>: Century Karting, Eastern Mezzanine Level, Canal Walk, 021 525 1720. Bounce World, Montague Drive, Montague Gardens, 021 552 3165. Gazoome, Marconi Centre, Koeberg Road, Milnerton, 021 837 1313 or 084 455 6722.

<u>Eat</u>: Century City Natural Goods Market, Park Lane, Central Park, Century City, 021 531 2173.

<u>Shop</u>: Canal Walk, Century Boulevard, Century City, 021 529 9600.

---

6 Ratanga Junction Theme Park

www.ratanga.co.za

5/5 Party venue rating

1/5 Rainy day option

With more than 30 attractions, including 23 rides for children, families and thrill-seekers alike, this is possibly the closest you can get to a real-life wonderland. Top scores for popularity go to the thrill rides, although some of these have a minimum height requirement, so check the website first. The Slingshot is a controlled freefall, Monkey Falls is a high log-flume ride and Cape Cobra is a looping rollercoaster. There are also many attractions that can be enjoyed as a family, such as Murphy's mini golf (a nine-hole indoor course), the snake park and a magic show. You can also see the Lego display.

COST R181 for those taller than 1.3m, R95 for those shorter than 1.3m, R70 for a fun pass, R55 per flight on the Slingshot

Tel number	021 550 8504
Address	Century Boulevard, Century City
GPS marker	33°53'50"S; 18°30'39"E
Closest public transport	Century City Railway Station, Metrorail and MyCiTi Bus route 251
Opening hours	Open seasonally, 10am–5pm
Most appropriate age group	8+
Pram/wheelchair-friendly	Yes
Baby-changing facility	Yes
Nearest hospital	Canal Walk Medical Centre, 021 552 8080
	Netcare N1 City Hospital, 021 590 4444

7 The White House Stables outride

thewhitehousestables.co.za

Spend a day on an outride and take a picnic to enjoy afterwards. The rides are guided and ideal for most families because groups are capped at four. These outrides head into the surrounding country area from Monday to Friday, and on some Sundays. The professional, family-owned equestrian centre is based in Morningstar. They also offer riding lessons on well-schooled horses for beginners to advanced riders (children and adults), and pony rides for the little ones, along with pony camps, livery, clinics and jumping, eventing and shows.

Take note: Sunday outrides are by prior arrangement, so be sure to book ahead of time.

Tel number	084 553 1556
Address	Corner Old Mamre and Zonnekus roads, Kernkrag
GPS marker	33°44'45"S; 18°32'21"E
Closest public transport	MyCiTi bus route 214 or 217
Opening hours	9am–4pm Monday to Friday, 9am–1pm Sunday
Most appropriate age group	7+
Pram/wheelchair-friendly	Yes, limited
Baby-changing facility	No
Nearest hospital	Netcare Blaauwberg Hospital, 021 554 9000

Nearby

Visit/see: Victory Paintball, off the R27 West Coast road, just outside Melkbos, 021 551 0884. SWAT Laser Tag, Melkbos 4x4 arena, R27, 074 188 8777.

Play/do: Color Me Crazy Den, Parklands, 021 554 4135.

Eat: Driftwood Café, corner Hamstead Close and Parklands Main Road, Parklands, 021 556 8897.

Shop: Bayside Mall, corner West Coast and Blaauwberg roads, Table View, 021 557 4350.

COST From R200 per person for one hour

Outside Cape Town

1. Blue Rock
2. Butterfly World
3. Cape Canopy Tour
4. Delvera Farm
5. Giraffe House Wildlife Awareness Centre
6. Graceland Venues
7. Helderberg Farm
8. Le Bonheur Croc Farm
9. Mariella's Restaurant, Capaia Wine Estate
10. West Coast Fossil Park
11. West Coast National Park
12. Wild Clover Farm

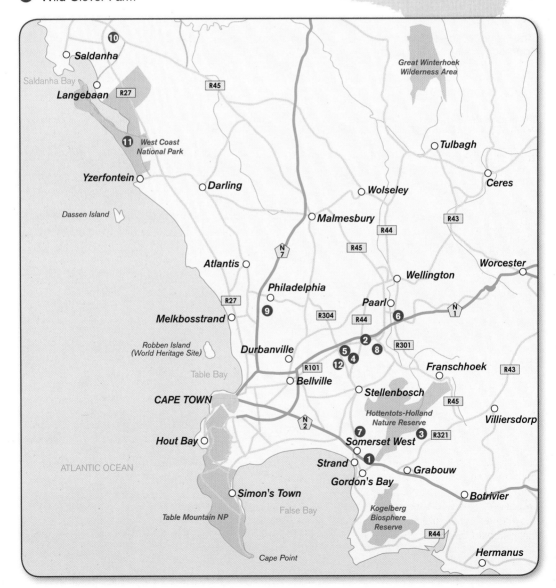

1 Blue Rock

www.bluerock.co.za

This is a supreme day out for the family in summer. Blue Rock Lake is the only clear-water lake in the Western Cape and offers cable water-skiing, kneeboarding and wakeboarding, which is skiing without using a motorboat – it's more social as your child's friends can watch him up close. The cable system can even speed up, allowing your adventurous child to ski barefoot. Blue Rock hires out shaded areas that overlook the lake as well as umbrellas, loungers, bean bags, deck chairs and floating mats. Add to this the excellent picnic facilities, a children's playground, a beach volleyball court, four swimming areas, rock jumping points into the lake, a foefie slide, paintball and diving location, and you'll wish this was an overnight spot.

Tel number	021 858 1330
Address	Sir Lowry's Pass Road, N2, Helderberg Rural
GPS marker	34°07'34"S; 18°54'20"E
Closest public transport	Somerset West Railway Station, Metrorail
Opening hours	10am–6pm daily December to January,
	10am–6pm Tuesday to Sunday, February to Easter,
	11am–5pm Saturday and Sunday, Easter to mid-June,
	Resort closed mid-June to mid-September,
	11am–5pm Tuesday to Sunday, mid-September to November
Most appropriate age group	6+
Pram/wheelchair-friendly	Yes
Baby-changing facility	Yes
Nearest hospital	Helderberg Hospital, 021 850 4700

Nearby
Visit/see:
Monkey Town,
Mondeor Road,
Somerset West,
021 858 1060.

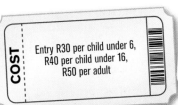

COST
Entry R30 per child under 6,
R40 per child under 16,
R50 per adult

---

2 Butterfly World

www.butterflyworld.co.za

Here families can view free-flying tropical butterflies that have been raised on breeding farms in countries such as Costa Rica, the Philippines and Malaysia. Butterfly World imports the pupae throughout the year, and the butterflies emerge into their tropical gardens. Besides housing butterflies, it also has a large aviary and a meerkat enclosure. There is a large iguana cage, and displays of indigenous and exotic spiders and scorpions. There is a gift shop, and the Jungle Leaf Café provides light meals and refreshments.

Take note:
On overcast days the butterflies are not active, which gives focus to other interesting animals.

Tel number	021 875 5628
Address	R44, Klapmuts
GPS marker	33°48'04"S; 18°52'19"E
Closest public transport	Stellenbosch Railway Station, Metrorail
Opening hours	9am–5pm daily
Most appropriate age group	3+
Pram/wheelchair-friendly	Yes
Baby-changing facility	Yes
Nearest hospital	Mediclinic Stellenbosch, 021 861 2000

COST: R65 per adult, R37 per child, R59 per pensioner, R167 per family ticket (two adults and two children)

3 Cape Canopy Tour
www.capecanopytour.co.za

 5/5 Party venue rating

 0/5 Rainy day option

Set among the cliffs, forest, waterfalls and diverse fynbos of a nature reserve in the scenic Elgin Valley, this fully guided nature experience consists of 13 platforms and slides up to 320m long. This zip-line canopy tour is guided and safe for all ages.

Tel number	021 300 0501
Address	Hottentots-Holland Nature Reserve, R321, Elgin
GPS marker	34°04'28"S; 19°03'43"E
Opening hours	8am–2pm
Most appropriate age group	5+
Pram/wheelchair-friendly	No
Baby-changing facility	No
Nearest hospital	Mediclinic Vergelegen, 021 850 9000

COST: R595 per person

Nearby

Visit/see: Oak Valley MTB Route, Oak Avenue, Elgin, 021 859 2510. Paul Cluver MTB route, De Rust Estate, N2, Grabouw, 021 844 0605.

Play/do: Mofam River Lodge (seasonal), Mofam Farm, Appletiser Road, 021 846 8345.

Eat: Platform 1 Eatery, Winters Drift, Oak Valley Road, 021 859 3354. Fresh, Paul Cluver Wine Estate, 071 563 6020. Pool Room, Oak Valley Estate, 021 859 4111. Gordon's Country Kitchen, Thandi Farm, 021 844 0343. The Gallery Restaurant, South Hill, The Valley, Grabouw, 021 844 0033.

Sleep: South Hill Guest House, The Valley, Grabouw, 021 844 0033. Old Mac Daddy, Elgin Valley, 021 844 0241.

For parents: Charles Fox Cap Classique Wine Estate, Valley Road, Elgin, 082 471 3444 or 082 569 2965.

Special events

Paul Cluver Forest Amphitheatre Summer Festival and Wines2Whales MTB Race

---

4 Delvera Farm
www.delvera.co.za

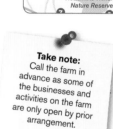

This agri-village has a host of activities geared towards children. Enjoy the BMX track and as a family explore the conservancy through hiking or mountain biking, or you can go on a guided full moon hike. Visit Funky Monkey children's creative centre, and for those of your children fascinated with how stuff works, there is a coin-operated mini train display with five working tracks that is a must-see for its intricate detail. There is also a party venue on site.

Take note: Call the farm in advance as some of the businesses and activities on the farm are only open by prior arrangement.

Tel number	021 884 4352
Address	R44, Stellenbosch
GPS marker	33°50'54"S; 18°51'31"E
Closest public transport	Stellenbosch Railway Station, Metrorail
Opening hours	8am–5pm daily
Most appropriate age group	2+
Pram/wheelchair-friendly	Yes
Baby-changing facility	Yes
Nearest hospital	Stellenbosch Mediclinic, 021 861 2000

Nearby

Visit/see: Stellenbosch Slow Market, Oude Libertas, Oude Libertas Road, Stellenbosch. Spier Wine Farm, R310 Baden Powell Road, Stellenbosch, 021 809 1100. Polkadraai Strawberry Farm, Lynedoch, Stellenbosch, 021 881 3854.

Play/do: Cookie Works, Dorp Street, Stellenbosch, 021 882 9775.

Eat: Lekke Neh, Weltevreden Wine Farm, Welgevonden Boulevard, Stellenbosch, 021 889 6588.

For parents: Pane E Vino, Dalla Cia, Lower Dorp Street, Bosman's Crossing, Stellenbosch, 021 883 8312.

Special events

There is a range of annual events to attend in the Stellenbosch region, including the annual Stellenbosch Wine Festival, a host of harvest festivals as well as the Stellenbosch Street Soiree and the Impi Challenge

5. Giraffe House Wildlife Awareness Centre

www.giraffehouse.co.za

 5/5 Party venue rating

 3/5 Rainy day option

The centre offers views of some of Africa's mammal, reptile and bird species. Along with a hand-reared giraffe, you can see zebra, ostrich, monkeys, warthog, caracal, eland, Nile crocodiles, tortoises and snakes. South Africa's national animal, the springbok, and the national bird, the blue crane, are also resident at the centre. Sharing trivia such as the giraffe being the tallest land animal on earth and the ostrich being the biggest bird, the wildlife education programme caters very well for children. Daily interactive encounters allow you to meet, touch and even hold some of the centre's interesting creatures. During one of the centre's wildlife talks you will learn what the smallest tortoise in the world looks like.

Tel number	021 884 4506
Address	R304 and R101
GPS marker	33°49'42"S; 18°48'00"E
Closest public transport	Stellenbosch Railway Station, Metrorail
Opening hours	9am–5pm daily
Most appropriate age group	2+
Pram/wheelchair-friendly	Yes
Baby-changing facility	Yes
Nearest hospital	Mediclinic Stellenbosch, 021 861 2000

COST R25 for 2–15-year-olds, R45 per adult and R30 per pensioner

6. Graceland Venues

www.graceland-venues.co.za

 5/5 Party venue rating

 1/5 Rainy day option

This family-oriented venue has four water slides and plenty of space for the young ones to run around. The day may be spent enjoying unlimited rides on the water slide, pool activities, unlimited use of the playpark with its tubes and tunnels, playing on the jungle gym and swings, and encounters with the farm animals, which are tortoises, pot-bellied pigs, geese, ducks, goats and chickens. Because the water slides are only open from October until the end of April, this is a summer day trip. Day visitors must contact them in advance to confirm availability.

Tel number	021 863 4109 or 072 264 4009
Address	Klein Dennegeur Farm, Lustigan Road, southern Paarl
GPS marker	33°44'56"S; 18°59'53"E
Closest public transport	Paarl Railway Station, Metrorail
Opening hours	9am–4pm Saturday, 10am–3pm Sunday, closed for day visitors from the end of April to the end of August
Most appropriate age group	7+
Pram/wheelchair-friendly	Yes
Baby-changing facility	Yes
Nearest hospital	Mediclinic Paarl, 021 807 8000

COST
R75 per child,
R100 per adult and
R50 for entrance only

7 Helderberg Farm
www.helderbergplaas.co.za

 5/5 Party venue rating

 2/5 Rainy day option

This farm really does offer a five-star family experience. Along with hiking trails, mountain biking, trail running and a 4×4 trail, there is a playground area in the tea garden. Children can go strawberry picking, there is a forest walk that is popular with older children, and there is a farmyard with chickens, rabbits, ducks and goats that can be fed with animal feed available to buy from the kiosk. The farm also offers combat games (paintball and laser tag). African drumming can be arranged in the amphitheatre, and Granny's Forest has a variety of picnic and braai sites.

Tel number	021 855 4308
Address	Klein Helderberg Road, Somerset West
GPS marker	34°01'59"S; 18°50'04"E
Closest public transport	Somerset West Railway Station, Metrorail
Opening hours	8am–6pm daily
Most appropriate age group	5+
Pram/wheelchair-friendly	Yes
Baby-changing facility	No
Nearest hospital	Mediclinic Vergelegen, 021 850 9000 Helderberg Hospital, 021 850 4700

Nearby
Sleep: NH The Lord Charles, corner Broadway Boulevard and Main Road, Heldervue, Somerset West, 021 855 1040.

COST
R30 for adults and
R20 for children

(8) Le Bonheur Croc Farm
www.lebonheurcrocfarm.co.za

 5/5 Party venue rating

 4/5 Rainy day option

Your children will love the farm's guided croc pond tour, conducted every 45 minutes, which leads across open dams that house over 1,000 crocodiles. Your child can touch a baby croc, and during the summer months watch a feeding. The café has many safe play areas for children, and you can prebook a picnic basket to enjoy on the lawns. There is a well-stocked dam for catch-and-release fishing, so take your own rod or rent one from the gift shop.

Tel number	021 863 1142
Address	Babylonstoren Road, R45, Simondium
GPS marker	33°49'05"S; 18°56'29"E
Closest public transport	Paarl Train Station, Metrorail
Opening hours	9am–5pm daily
Most appropriate age group	2+
Pram/wheelchair-friendly	Yes
Baby-changing facility	Yes
Nearest hospital	Mediclinic Paarl, 021 807 8000

Nearby
Visit/see: Babylonstoren, R45, Simondium, 084 275 1243.
Play/do: Paarl Rock Abseil, Cascade Country Manor, Waterval Road, Nederburg, Paarl, 021 868 0227.
Eat: Rhebokskloof Wine Estate, Windmeul, Agter-Paarl Road, 021 869 8386.
Shop: Spice Route, Suid Agter-Paarl Road, Paarl South, 021 863 5222.
Sleep: Berg River Resort, R45, Franschhoek Road, Paarl South, 021 007 1852. Lekkerwijn Country Guest House, R45, Franschhoek, 021 874 1122.

COST
R48 for adults and R28 for children under 18

Take note:
Call ahead for crocodile feeding times.

9 Mariella's Restaurant, Capaia Wine Estate
www.capaia.eu/restaurant

Take in a bit of the Swartland from the deck of Mariella's at Capaia Wine Estate while the children play on the lawn and jungle gym. Prepare to enjoy your meal with some good wine.

Tel number	021 972 1103
Address	Botterberg Road, Philadelphia
GPS marker	33°42'07"S; 18°34'25"E
Opening hours	11am–3pm Tuesday and Thursday, 11am–10pm Wednesday, Friday and Saturday, 11am–5pm Sunday
Most appropriate age group	6+
Pram/wheelchair-friendly	Yes
Baby-changing facility	Yes
Nearest hospital	Melkbos Clinic, 021 553 2499

Nearby
Eat: De Malle Meul (for Sunday buffet), Philadelphia, 021 972 1097.

10 West Coast Fossil Park
www.fossilpark.org.za

Go on a tour to see the fossils of bears, sabre-toothed cats, short-necked giraffes and other exotic animals that inhabited the West Coast around five million years ago. There is a children's playpark in a garden area that is also great for picnics – pack your own or order one in advance from the coffee shop. If you're an active or outdoorsy family, there are four MTB trails open, ranging from 3.5km to 10km. For hikers there is a scenic 3.5km nature trail.

Tel number	022 766 1606
Address	R45 Langebaanweg, Vredenburg
GPS marker	32°57'30"S; 18°07'23"E
Opening hours	8am–4pm weekdays, weekend hours vary according to the season (enquire directly)
Most appropriate age group	6+
Pram/wheelchair-friendly	Yes
Baby-changing facility	No
Nearest hospital	Life West Coast Private Hospital, 022 719 1030

Call for fees,
under 5s are free

COST

---

11 West Coast National Park

www.sanparks.co.za

5/5 Party venue rating

2/5 Rainy day option

For fit families with older children, Eve's Trail is a great two-and-a-half-day, fully portered and catered hike through the park, which is offered by the Cape West Coast Biosphere Reserve. There is naturally plenty more for families keen on easy walks, mountain biking, kayaking and kiteboarding on the Langebaan Lagoon, picnics and braais at the custom-built facilities and, if you time it well, spotting whales in August and September from Atlantic View Point, the Tsaarsbank section and the Plankiesbaai section of the park.

Take note:
The Wild Card comes highly recommended if you visit many of the SANParks.

Tel number	022 772 2144
Address	Main Street, Langebaan
GPS marker	33°14'38"S; 18°12'16"E
Opening hours	Visit the website
Most appropriate age group	6+
Pram/wheelchair-friendly	Yes
Baby-changing facility	No
Nearest hospital	Life West Coast Private Hospital, 022 719 1030

Visit their website

COST

Nearby
Eat: Die Strandloper, on the beach, Langebaan, 022 772 2490
Sleep: Duinepos, West Coast National Park, 022 707 9900 or 083 704 7067.
Abrahamskraal, West Coast National Park, 022 772 2144/5.
The Farmhouse Hotel, Langebaan Lagoon, 022 772 2062.

Special event
The flower season occurs in August and September every year

 **12** # Wild Clover Farm
www.wildclover.co.za

 4/5 Party venue rating   3/5 Rainy day option

This family-focused farm with its expansive pastures and whitewashed fences also has a restaurant and children's play area. The farm offers archery, clay pigeon shooting and a brewery. The restaurant provides high chairs and offers smaller portions for little diners. Set up in the shade of the oak trees while the children play safely in the children's zone – there is an 80m push-bike track around the garden and a jungle gym with swings, monkey bars and a slide. There is also a 'pops and tots' cycle track, which entails a gentle 4km off-road route around the farm. A section of the track runs alongside the neighbouring Villiera Wildlife Sanctuary, which is home to plains game, an abundance of birds and a pair of giraffe.

Tel number	021 865 2248
Address	R304, Stellenbosch
GPS marker	33°50'51"S; 18°48'12"E
Closest public transport	Stellenbosch Railway Station, Metrorail
Opening hours	2pm–10pm Tuesday to Thursday, 9am–10pm Friday and Saturday, 9am–4pm Sunday
Most appropriate age group	2+
Pram/wheelchair-friendly	Yes
Baby-changing facility	Yes
Nearest hospital	Netcare Kuils River Private Hospital, 021 900 6000

Special event
The family-friendly festival, Famfest, is hosted here

Getting around Durban

To get around Durban, you can hire a car from companies such as Avis, Europcar and Bidvest Car Rental. Taxi services are also available, with Uber and Mozzie Cabs being two reliable services.

Some of the areas through which you travel can be busy, which may make them crime hotspots. Be vigilant and lock your doors while driving, use secure parking, and ensure your car is locked when leaving it.

Car rentals
Avis, 0861 021 111
Europcar, 0861 131 000
Bidvest Car Rental, 086 101 7722

Taxi cabs
Uber (download the app), www.uber.com
Mozzie Cabs, 031 303 5787

Central Durban

- ❶ African Art Centre
- ❷ CROW
- ❸ Durban Botanic Gardens
- ❹ KZNSA Art Gallery
- ❺ Mini Town
- ❻ Moses Mabhida Stadium
- ❼ Port Natal Maritime Museum
- ❽ uMgeni River Bird Park
- ❾ uShaka Marine World

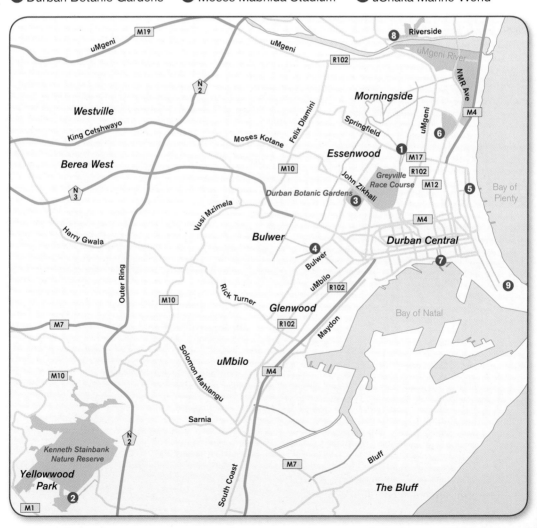

1 African Art Centre
www.afriart.org.za

This vibrant art centre collects, displays and sells artwork created by disadvantaged communities. Some of these products include telephone-wire baskets, traditional Zulu ceramics, antique Zulu beadwork and beaded jewellery. On occasion, the crafters are present at the centre, where you can see them at work.

Tel number	031 312 3804
Address	94 Florida Road, Morningside
GPS marker	29°50'07"S; 31°01'06"E
Opening hours	8:30am–5pm Monday to Friday, 9am–3pm Saturday
Most appropriate age group	10+
Pram/wheelchair-friendly	No
Baby-changing facility	No
Nearest hospital	Netcare Parklands Hospital, 031 242 4000
	Netcare St Augustine's Hospital, 031 268 5000
	Life Entabeni Hospital, 031 204 1377

Nearby
Visit/see: Jameson Park, 350 Montpelier Road, 031 303 2275. Mitchell Park Zoo, 10 Ferndale Road, 031 303 2275.
Eat: Blue Zoo Café, 6 Nimmo Road, 031 303 3568. Wakaberry, 217 Florida Road, 031 312 8711.

Take note:
There is limited parking near the centre; rather park on Florida Road and stroll down.

Take note:
There is fragile artwork on display, which older children may appreciate. Avoid taking younger children here.

---

2 CROW
www.crowkzn.co.za

The Centre for Rehabilitation of Wildlife aims to help care for and rehabilitate wild animals. For the public, there is a monthly open day, where visitors can see and learn about the animals. Animals at the centre include monkeys, baboons, birds of prey and antelopes. Talks and presentations can be arranged, and holiday programmes are often available.

Take note:
There are stairs to the raptor enclosure, but everywhere else is pram-friendly.

Tel number	031 462 1127
	083 212 5281 (after hours)
Address	15A Coedmore Avenue, Yellowwood Park
GPS marker	29°55'10"S; 30°56'10"E
Opening hours	Open days: 11am–1pm, last Sunday of the month; private tours for special-interest groups and schools can be arranged
Most appropriate age group	4+
Pram/wheelchair-friendly	Yes
Baby-changing facility	No
Nearest hospital	Life Westville Hospital, 031 251 6911 Netcare St Augustine's Hospital, 031 268 5000

Nearby

Visit/see: Bergtheil Museum, 16 Queens Avenue, Westville, 031 203 7107. The Pavilion, Jack Martens Drive, 031 275 9800.
Play/do: Southern Rock Climbing Gym, 5 Valley View Road, New Germany, 031 705 3842.
Eat: Marula's, 112 Maryvale Road, 031 266 7600. Chez Nous, Westville Junction, 031 266 7011. John Dory's, Village Market Shopping Centre, Westville, 031 266 0184.
Shop: The Toy Factory Shop, 119 Pinecrest Centre, Pinetown, 031 701 2968.

COST — Open days: adults R25, children R10

 Durban Botanic Gardens
www.durbanbotanicgardens.org.za

 2/5 Party venue rating

 0/5 Rainy day option

These beautifully kept gardens offer a breath of fresh air in the heart of Durban. Pathways, wide-open lawns, a small lake teeming with birdlife, and a selection of themed gardens can all be seen at this venue. The themed gardens include an orchid house, a herb garden, fern and cycad gardens, and a garden of the senses. Take a picnic or enjoy something from the tea garden. Regular concerts are held at the lake, and these accommodate children as well, with a special KidZone. Educational programmes are also available.

Take note:
You can have parties here but equipment, such as a jumping castle, is not allowed. Parking is available at the main entrance or at the tea garden entrance on John Zikhali Road.

Tel number	031 309 9240
	031 201 2766 (tea garden)
Address	9A John Zikhali Road, Durban
GPS marker	29°50'49"S; 31°00'35"E
Opening hours	Open daily; in summer (16 September to 15 April) from 7:30am–5:45pm and in winter (16 April to 15 September) from 7:30am–5:15pm; Orchid House: 9am–5pm; information office: 8am–4:30pm; tea garden: 10am–4pm Monday, 9am–4pm Tuesday to Sunday, closed on Christmas Day and Good Friday
Most appropriate age group	1+
Pram/wheelchair-friendly	Yes
Baby-changing facility	Yes
Nearest hospital	Netcare St Augustine's Hospital, 031 268 5000
	Netcare Parklands Hospital, 031 242 4000

Nearby

Play/do: Artbeat Studios, 656 Musgrave Road, 031 209 3710.
Eat: Chateau Gateaux, 136 Problem Mkhize Road, 031 309 1661.
Shop: Essenwood Market (every Saturday), Stephen Dlamini Road, 031 208 1264. Keachea, Musgrave Shopping Centre, 031 201 5502.
For parents: 9th Avenue Bistro, Shop 2, Avonmore Centre, 031 312 9134.

COST: Free entry; concert prices vary, depending on performers

---

4 KZNSA Art Gallery
www.kznsagallery.co.za

0/5 Party venue rating
2/5 Rainy day option

This art gallery has the Main, Mezzanine and Park galleries in which exhibits from a variety of artists are hosted. A cinema also caters for digital projections, and the shop provides an outlet for local craft. The Arts Café offers a selection of dishes for adults and children, and boasts a children's play area.

Take note:
On weekends, children's entertainment is available at the café.

Tel number	031 277 1705
	031 277 1700 (shop)
Address	166 Bulwer Road, Glenwood
GPS marker	29°51'37"S; 30°59'49"E
Opening hours	9am–5pm Tuesday to Friday, 9am–4pm Saturday, 10am–3pm Sunday and public holidays, closed on Mondays
Most appropriate age group	3+
Pram/wheelchair-friendly	No
Baby-changing facility	Yes
Nearest hospital	Netcare St Augustine's Hospital, 031 268 5000
	Life Entabeni Hospital, 031 204 1377

Nearby

Visit/see: Phansi Museum, 500 Esther Roberts Road, 031 206 2889.
Eat: Glenwood Bakery, 398 Esther Roberts Road, 031 205 0217. Olive and Oil, corner Helen Joseph and Bulwer roads, 031 201 6146. The Corner Café, 197 Brand Road, 031 201 0219.
For parents: The Factory Café, 369 Magwaza Maphalala Street, 031 205 3283.

Special events

Literary and art-themed festivals that run every year include the Time of the Writer in March, the Durban International Film Festival in July, Jomba! Contemporary Dance Experience in August or September, and Poetry Africa in October

5 Mini Town

4/5 Party venue rating

0/5 Rainy day option

This miniature version of Durban gives visitors a different perspective of the city. It contains small replicas of signature buildings in the city, such as the sugar terminals and City Hall, and features a working model train and shipyard.

Tel number	031 337 7892
Address	114 Snell Parade, Durban Beachfront
GPS marker	29°50'41"S; 31°02'08"E
Opening hours	9:30am–4:30pm daily
Most appropriate age group	2+
Pram/wheelchair-friendly	Yes
Baby-changing facility	No
Nearest hospital	Netcare Parklands Hospital, 031 242 4000
	Netcare St Augustine's Hospital, 031 268 5000
	Life Entabeni Hospital, 031 204 1377

Take note:
There is parking available near the entrance.

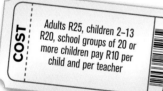

COST Adults R25, children 2–13 R20, school groups of 20 or more children pay R10 per child and per teacher

Nearby
Visit/see: The Amphitheatre Gardens on the beachfront has a flea market every Sunday.
Play/do: On Durban's beachfront you can swim, play in the sand, and ride your bike or skateboard. The Ricksha Bus offers tours of the city in an open-top double-decker bus. The office is at North Beach, 031 322 4209. The Skate Store is next to the Skate Park, 90 Snell Parade, Durban Beachfront, 031 337 9270. Suncoast Casino, Suncoast Boulevard, Marine Parade, 031 328 3000.
Eat: Circus, Circus Beach Café, Shop 1, Snell Parade, 031 337 7700.

Special event
The ECR House and Garden Show takes place every year from late June to early July

6 Moses Mabhida Stadium
www.mmstadium.com

 4/5 Party venue rating
 2/5 Rainy day option

Built for the FIFA World Cup™ in 2010, this stadium has become more than just a venue for games. Apart from the restaurants and shops at its base, organised activities are also available. These include stadium tours, climbing the steps of the arch, riding in the Sky Car to the viewing platform at the top of the arch and, for older thrill-seekers, jumping off the arch in the Big Rush Big Swing. The People's Park, located at the base of the steps, is ideal for families, with its wide walkways for riding bikes, the extensive play area, and the café, which offers a variety of meals to suit most tastes. Segway tours are also available from the stadium.

Tel number	031 582 8242
	031 303 5719 (People's Park)
Address	44 Isaiah Ntshangase Road, Durban
GPS marker	29°49'44"S; 31°01'49"E
Opening hours	Visitor Centre opens 9am–5pm daily; Sky Car: 9am–5pm, Big Rush Big Swing (weather dependent): 10am–4pm Friday to Monday and Wednesday, stadium tours: 9am–4pm daily, adventure walk: 10am, 1pm and 3pm weekends only; People's Park café: 7am–5pm Monday to Friday, 7am–6pm Saturday and Sunday
Most appropriate age group	4+
Pram/wheelchair-friendly	Yes
Baby-changing facility	Yes
Nearest hospital	Netcare Parklands Hospital, 031 242 4000
	Netcare St Augustine's Hospital, 031 268 5000

Nearby

Visit/see: ArtSpace Durban, 3 Millar Road, 031 312 0793. I Heart Market, Moses Mabhida Stadium. Street Scene Tours, 39 Station Drive, 031 321 5079.
Play/do: Kings Park Swimming Pool, 43 Walter Gilbert Road, 031 312 0404. Segway tours, Moses Mabhida Stadium, 031 303 4534.
Shop: Stables Lifestyle Market, Jacko Jackson Drive, 031 312 3752.

COST Sky Car: adults R60, children under 12 R30, pensioners R55, children under 6 free, scholars on school tour R30; Big Swing: R695, no children under 10; stadium tours: adults R50, children under 12 R25, children under 6 free, pensioners R40; Adventure Walk: R90, pensioners R80, no children under 10

Special event
The Amashova Durban Classic takes place in October each year; cyclists race from Pieter-maritzburg or Hillcrest down to Durban

Take note: You are not allowed to take your own food and drinks into the stadium. Wi-Fi is available at People's Park.

7 Port Natal Maritime Museum

www.durban-history.co.za

Durban's maritime past, and the influence it has had on Durban itself, comes to light in these exhibitions, which are housed in out-of-commission vessels. These include a steam tugboat and a mine-sweeper, which visitors can explore, and from which you can look out over Durban's harbour.

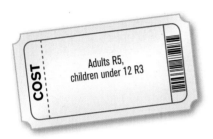

COST: Adults R5, children under 12 R3

Tel number	031 311 2231
Address	Maritime Place, Durban
GPS marker	29°51'43"S; 31°01'43"E
Opening hours	8:30am–4pm Monday to Saturday, 11am–4pm Sundays and public holidays
Most appropriate age group	6+
Pram/wheelchair-friendly	No
Baby-changing facility	No
Nearest hospital	Netcare St Augustine's Hospital, 031 268 5000 Life Entabeni Hospital, 031 204 1377

Take note: Parking is available next to the museum. Large groups should book in advance. Portable toilets are provided.

Nearby
Visit/see: Catalina Theatre, Wilson's Wharf, 031 837 5999. Playhouse Theatre, 231 Anton Lembede Street, 031 369 9555. Durban Art Gallery and Durban Natural Science Museum in the City Hall, 234 Anton Lembede Street, 031 311 2264, 031 311 2256.
Play/do: Durban Harbour cruises are available from private charter companies.
Eat: You can shop and eat at Wilson's Wharf, where there is an indoor flea market and various casual restaurants, 14–18 Boatmans Road, 031 907 8792.

Special event
The South African Women's Arts Festival runs at the Playhouse Theatre during August

8 uMgeni River Bird Park

www.umgeniriverbirdpark.co.za

Situated next to the uMgeni River, the park is home to over 800 birds from 200 species. Visitors can walk through the park, learning about birds and their different environments. There are free-flight bird shows, as well as a café that offers light meals and refreshments and also has a playground.

Tel number	031 579 4601
	031 579 3377 (The Cockatoo Café)
Address	490 Riverside Road, Durban North
GPS marker	29°48'31"S; 31°01'04"E
Opening hours	9am–5pm daily, closed Christmas Day;
	show times are at 11am and 2pm Tuesday to Sunday
Most appropriate age group	4+
Pram/wheelchair-friendly	Yes
Baby-changing facility	Yes
Nearest hospital	Netcare Parklands Hospital, 031 242 4000
	Ethekwini Hospital and Heart Centre, 031 581 2400

Nearby

Visit/see: Durban Green Corridor's Green Hub, 31 Stiebel Place, 031 322 6026. Beachwood Mangroves Nature Reserve, Riverside Road, 083 293 3611.
Sleep: Riverside Hotel, 10 Kenneth Kaunda Road, 031 563 0600.

COST
Adults R50, children 4–12 years and pensioners R30, children under 4 free

Special event

The Dusi Canoe Marathon, every February, sees the final leg coming down the uMgeni into the lagoon

---

9 uShaka Marine World
www.ushakamarineworld.co.za

5/5 Party venue rating

2/5 Rainy day option

This marine theme park consists of several areas, starting with the Village Walk, which has a number of family-friendly restaurants, shops selling an assortment of beach gear, clothes and souvenirs, and Dangerous Creatures, where you can see snakes, spiders and other venomous creatures. Sea World, the aquarium, housed in an upside-down ship, is home to a variety of sea life and marine animals. The water park has slides and rides to suit everyone, from little children to older thrill-seekers. Lastly, uShaka Kids World caters specifically for children 2–10 years old and has all sorts of activities to keep them busy.

Take note:
Food hampers, braais and cooler boxes are not allowed within the uShaka Marine World premises. You can hire out lockers in the water park.

Tel number	031 328 8000
Address	1 King Shaka Avenue, Point
GPS marker	29°52'04"S; 31°02'44"E
Opening hours	Wet 'n Wild: 9am–5pm daily in peak season, 10am–5pm Wednesday to Sunday in the off-peak season; Sea World: 9am–5pm daily; Kids World: 9am–5pm daily in peak season, and Wednesday to Sunday in the off-peak season; Dangerous Creatures: 10am–5pm daily in peak season, 10am–4:30pm in the off-peak season; The Village Walk: 9am–6pm daily

COST
Wet 'n Wild and Sea World: ticket prices vary; Kids World: adults R20, children 2–12 years R65, children under 2 free; Dangerous Creatures: R45, children under 2 free; Chimp & Zee Rope Adventure: R150 per person, minimum height of 1.2m; Village Walk: free entry

Most appropriate age group	1+
Pram/wheelchair-friendly	Yes
Baby-changing facility	Yes
Nearest hospital	Netcare St Augustine's Hospital, 031 268 5000
	Life Entabeni Hospital, 031 204 1377

Nearby
<u>Play/do</u>: Ocean Ventures, uShaka Marine World, 086 100 1138.
Roxy Learn 2 Surf, Addington Beach, 076 877 5143.
Learn 2 Surf, Addington Beach, SMS 083 414 0567.
<u>For parents</u>: Wahooz on the Promenade, uShaka Marine World, 031 328 8000.

Special event
The Discovery ECR Big Walk takes place in May, and sees walkers taking different routes from uShaka Marine World to Moses Mabhida Stadium

North Coast

1. Burnedale
2. Flag Animal Farm
3. Gateway Theatre of Shopping
4. Hingham Nursery
5. KZN Sharks Board
6. Lucky Linton Gold Mine
7. Sugar Rush
8. uMhlanga Promenade

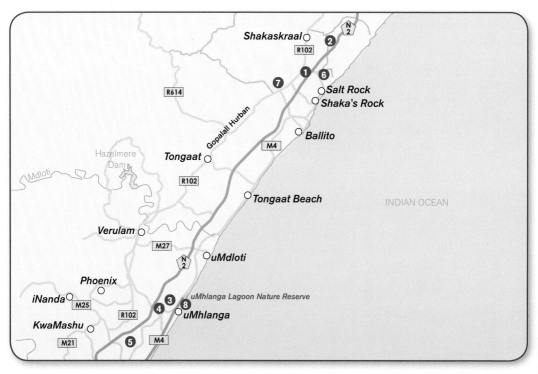

1 Burnedale

www.burnedale.co.za

This charming centre offers a collection of venues at which guests can eat, play or shop. The café is near to the play area, and children can also see farm animals. Creative workshops are available for adults, who can also browse through various children's clothing and décor boutique stores.

Tel number	032 947 0133 (café)
Address	1 Old Main Road, uMhlali
GPS marker	29°28'50"S; 31°13'17"E
Opening hours	Café: 8:30am–4:30pm daily; shop hours vary, and some shops are closed on Mondays
Most appropriate age group	1–11
Pram/wheelchair-friendly	Yes
Baby-changing facility	Yes
Nearest hospital	Netcare Alberlito Hospital, 032 946 6700

Nearby
Visit/see: The Litchi Orchard, Seaforth Drive, 032 525 5118.
Play/do: Happi Days, Sage Centre, 032 525 8059.
Eat: Sage Café, 1 Old Fort Road, 032 525 8059.
For parents: Green Food Studio and Mangwanani Spa, Boulevard 44 Boutique Hotel, 44 Lee Barns Boulevard, 032 947 1660.

Take note:
The baby-changing facility is in the last cubicle in the ladies' restroom. The playground near the café is for younger children, but another playground for older children is available.

COST: Free entry; playground R10 per child (children 0–5) payable to One of a Kind

---

2 Flag Animal Farm

www.flaganimalfarm.co.za

This popular animal farm is home to over 1,000 rescued or unwanted animals and birds, including cows, horses, goats and reptiles. This family-orientated venue offers daily milking shows, a chance to hand-feed baby animals, enjoy pony rides, train rides, play-grounds, an indoor play centre with jungle gyms, sandpits, an obstacle course, and more to keep children entertained. You can take a picnic, have a braai, or have a light bite to eat at the tea garden. School excursions are welcome, and 36-bed accommodation is available. There are also birthday party venues and a conference room.

Take note:
You are welcome to take in your own food. Baby-changing facilities are available in the men's and ladies' restrooms.

Tel number	032 947 2018
Address	Sheffield Beach Road, Sheffield beach
GPS marker	29°27'04"S; 31°14'29"E
Most appropriate age group	1+
Opening hours	9am–4:30pm daily; wolf interaction: 11am daily; milking shows and bottle feedings: 12pm and 3pm daily; reptile show: 1:30pm daily
Pram/wheelchair-friendly	Yes
Baby-changing facility	Yes
Nearest hospital	Netcare Alberlito Hospital, 032 946 6700

Nearby

Play/do: Club Venture, off Esenembe Road, 032 942 8014. Holla Trails, Collisheen, 082 899 3114.

Sleep: Rain Farm Game Lodge, near Esenembe Road, 032 815 1050. Cane Cutters Resort, Douglas Crowe Drive, 032 947 0851. Sugar Bay, further up the coast at Zinkwazi Beach, offers children's camps, 21 Nkwazi Drive, 032 485 3778.

COST — Entrance is R39, children from 18 months pay the same; pony and train rides are R10 and animal feeds and carrots are R10 per packet

 Gateway Theatre of Shopping

www.gatewayworld.co.za

0/5 Party venue rating **5/5** Rainy day option

Come rain or shine, there is always something to do at the Gateway complex. The Wavehouse offers experienced and novice surfers and bodyboarders a chance to take on the waves. Inside there is a range of entertainment options, including a cinema complex, rides, arcade games, go-karting and putt putt. Get something to eat or enjoy a cup of coffee at one of the many restaurants or food outlets situated throughout the centre. And, of course, there is shopping aplenty, with a range of boutique and department stores available for the most discerning shopper.

Tel number	031 514 0500 0861 428 3929
Address	1 Palm Boulevard, uMhlanga Ridge, New Town Centre
GPS marker	29°43'51"S; 31°04'04"E
Opening hours	9am–7pm Monday to Thursday, 9am–9pm Friday and Saturday, 9am–6pm Sunday
Most appropriate age group	4+
Pram/wheelchair-friendly	Yes
Baby-changing facility	Yes
Nearest hospital	Netcare uMhlanga Hospital, 031 560 5500 Gateway Private Hospital, 031 492 1130

Nearby

<u>Visit/see</u>: Barnyard Theatre on the Palm Boulevard, first floor, Gateway Theatre of Shopping, 031 566 3045.
<u>Play/do</u>: Build-a-Bear, Gateway Theatre of Shopping, 08611 BEARS (23277). Action Karting, Electric Avenue, Gateway Theatre of Shopping, 031 566 2247. The Wavehouse, Gateway Theatre of Shopping, 031 584 9400. Mr Funtubbles, Palm Court Boulevard, Gateway Theatre of Shopping

<u>Eat</u>: Col'Cacchio, ground floor, Gateway Theatre of Shopping, 031 584 6822. Old Town Italy, 39 Meridian Drive, uMhlanga, 031 566 5008.

Take note:
There is no payment for parking tickets at the exit; payment must be made before you leave. Shopping hours are extended over the festive season.

---

④ Hingham Nursery
www.hinghamnursery.co.za

 0/5 Party venue rating

 2/5 Rainy day option

You can find a variety of indigenous plants, seedlings, herbs and garden products as well as a tea garden that offers an assortment of light lunches and tea treats. There is a play area for children and a thatch roof to provide shade or shelter. The nursery also boasts a gift shop.

Tel number	031 564 3062 074 141 5776
Address	15 Clematis Grove, Glenhills, off Rinaldo Road
GPS marker	29°45'40"S; 31°01'58"E
Opening hours	Nursery: 8am–4:30pm Monday to Saturday, 8:30am–4:30pm Sundays and public holidays; tea garden: 8:30am–4pm Tuesday to Sunday
Most appropriate age group	2–8
Pram/wheelchair-friendly	Yes, most places, but not everywhere
Baby-changing facility	Yes
Nearest hospital	Ethekwini Hospital and Heart Centre, 031 581 2400

Take note:
The tea garden is open on public holidays that fall on a Monday.

Nearby

<u>Visit/see</u>: La Lucia Library, 1 Library Lane, 031 572 2986.
<u>Play/do</u>: Durban Society of Model Engineers, 10 Hinton Grove, Virginia, 031 205 1089. SWAT Laser Tag, Durban North, 076 444 5570.
<u>Eat</u>: The Coffee Corner, 20 Mackeurtan Avenue, 031 563 0882. Apache River Spur, 12 Radar Drive, 031 564 3368. Kupcake Heaven, 99 uMhlanga Rocks Drive, 031 564 3993.
<u>Shop</u>: The Carnival Toys and Gifts, Northway Shopping Centre, 031 573 1591. Golden Hours Family Market, corner Uitsig Road and Radar Drive, 083 262 3693. The Food Market, 6 High Grove, 083 303 2517.

⑤ KZN Sharks Board
www.shark.co.za

Learners can see dynamic audiovisual shows and shark dissections, or they can walk through the Shark Museum, where they will see life-size replicas of sharks and other marine animals. Boat trips out to sea are also available.

Tel number	031 566 0400
	082 403 9206 (boat tour bookings)
Address	1A Herrwood Drive, uMhlanga
GPS marker	29°43'17"S; 31°04'33"E
Opening hours	Shark dissections: 9am and 2pm Tuesday to Thursday, and 2pm first Sunday of the month; boat tours last two hours and run at 6:30am Monday to Friday; museum: 8am–4pm Monday to Friday, 1pm–4pm first Sunday of the month
Most appropriate age group	5+
Pram/wheelchair-friendly	Yes
Baby-changing facility	No
Nearest hospital	Netcare uMhlanga Hospital, 031 560 5500 Gateway Private Hospital, 031 492 1130

COST Shark dissections: adults R45, children and pensioners R25; boat tours: R300 per person

Nearby
Play/do: Funky Monkey, 7 Tetford Circle, 031 566 2000.
Shop: Wonder Market, Chris Saunders Park, 079 747 7661.
Sleep: Coastlands uMhlanga, 329 uMhlanga Rocks Drive, 031 514 6500.

Take note: Sunday shows may change; contact the office to confirm.

⑥ Lucky Linton Gold Mine
www.luckylinton.com

Children learn to pan for gold in the genuine gold mine at this picnic and play venue. There is a dam where you can fish for bass, an animal farm where you can feed the animals, pony rides, foefie slides, a play gym and tree swings. There is also a scratch patch with semiprecious stones. You can take your own picnic, or braai at the venue while your children run around on the wide lawns. The venue is available for school outings and birthday parties as well. Accommodation is available in the bush caravan park, Linton House or Linton Cottage.

Tel number	083 255 1277
	032 947 1459
Address	Glendale Road, Shakaskraal, uMhlali
GPS marker	29°26'12"S; 31°11'43"E
Opening hours	8am–4pm daily
Most appropriate age group	3+
Pram/wheelchair-friendly	Yes
Baby-changing facility	No
Nearest hospital	Netcare Alberlito Hospital, 032 946 6700

Nearby

Play/do: Tidal Tao Snorkel Safaris, Shaka's Rock, 079 307 0608.

Sleep: Salt Rock Hotel, Hotel Road, 032 525 5025. Canelands Beach Club and Spa (also has a restaurant), 2 Shrimp Lane, 032 525 2300.

COST: Entry R20; scratch patch R2 per stone

---

(7) Sugar Rush

www.sugarrush.co.za

 5/5 Party venue rating

 1/5 Rainy day option

While this is a mountain-biking park with a network of trails nearby, it also caters for families. There is a coffee shop, where you will find a variety of refreshments, a play area, wide-open spaces and a Floriculture Centre, where you can get cut flowers. The venue also caters for children's parties.

Take note:
Hot showers, toilets, and a bike wash are available. Children under 16 must be accompanied by an adult on the external trails. Closed shoes and riding helmets must be worn on the MTB routes.

COST: MTB day pass R40; MTB session card (10 rides) R300; trail running R15; children's MTB and pump track R30

Tel number	087 351 2954
	079 232 9101
Address	Esenembe Road, Collisheen Estate, Ballito
GPS marker	29°29'30"S; 31°10'50"E
Opening hours	Gates open 5:30am–5pm in summer (October to March), and 6am–5pm in winter (April to September)
	The Sugar Rush Café is open 7am–4pm Wednesday to Sunday
Most appropriate age group	5+
Pram/wheelchair-friendly	Yes
Baby-changing facility	No
Nearest hospital	Netcare Alberlito Hospital, 032 946 6700

Nearby

Visit/see: Crocodile Creek, off Greylands Road, Maidstone, 082 920 0730. Ndlondlo Reptile Park, Asgard Estate, 073 753 1495. The Barn Swallows, Mt Moreland near uMdloti, 031 568 1557.
Eat: John Dory's, Ballito Lifestyle Centre, 032 946 3009. Mozambik, Boulevard Centre, 032 946 0979.
Sleep: Fairmont Zimbali Resort, Fairmont Estate, Zimbali, 032 538 5000.

Special event

Mr Price Pro Ballito takes place in July, and visitors can expect surfing and entertainment

---

8 uMhlanga Promenade

www.umhlangatourism.co.za

Stretching along the sunny beaches and warm seas of uMhlanga is the bricked promenade, from which visitors have easy access to the beaches. Beach festivals often take place during holidays, offering a variety of family-friendly activities.

Tel number	031 561 4257 (uMhlanga Tourism)
Address	Lagoon Drive, uMhlanga
GPS marker	29°43'42"S; 31°05'17"E
Most appropriate age group	3+
Pram/wheelchair-friendly	Yes
Baby-changing facility	No
Nearest hospital	Netcare uMhlanga Hospital, 031 560 5500
	Gateway Private Hospital, 031 492 1130

Take note:
Take a little cash for refreshments or purchases from vendors. If you're walking here in the evening or at night, do so in groups.

Nearby

Visit/see: uMhlanga Lagoon Nature Reserve, Hawaan, 031 561 2271. The uMhlanga lighthouse outside the Oyster Box Hotel.
Sleep: Oyster Box Hotel, 2 Lighthouse Road, 031 514 5000.
For parents: Bamboo Sushi Lounge, 17 Chartwell Drive, 031 561 2705.

Special events

The uMhlanga Summer Carnival in December and the uMhlanga July Festival in July take place at the beach and surrounding areas

South Coast

1. Crocworld Conservation Centre
2. Galleria Ice Rink
3. Splash Waterworld

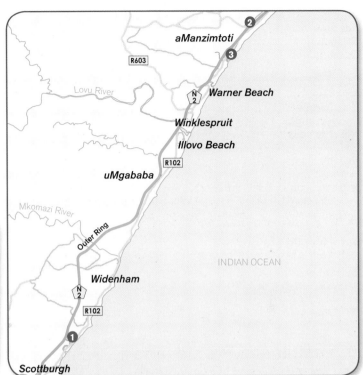

 Crocworld Conservation Centre

5/5 Party venue rating

1/5 Rainy day option

www.crocworld.co.za

This park is open every day and is home to a variety of wildlife, most impressive of which is the crocodiles. Children can get up close to these ancient animals and learn about them first hand. There is an animal farm, walk-through bird aviary, and daily crocodile feedings and snake demonstrations. Educational resources make the centre ideal for school groups and children who want to learn about nature. The landscaped indigenous garden provides a tranquil setting from which you can see the ocean. Visitors can also make use of the restaurant, open until 3pm daily.

Take note:
Guests eating at Le Rendez-Vous Restaurant do not pay the entrance fee unless they wish to access the park.

Tel number	039 976 1103
Address	Old Main Road, Scottburgh
GPS marker	30°15'22"S; 30°46'15"E
Opening hours	Open daily 8am–4:30pm out of season, and 8am–5pm during holidays; crocodile feedings: 11am and 3pm; snake demonstrations: 10:15am daily in season and 11:30am Saturday and Sunday out of season; restaurant: 9am–3pm daily
Most appropriate age group	4+
Pram/wheelchair-friendly	Yes
Baby-changing facility	Yes
Nearest hospital	GJ Crookes Hospital, 039 978 7000 Netcare Kingsway Hospital, 031 904 7000

Nearby

Play/do: Shark Cage Diving KZN, Landers Dive Centre, Rocky Bay, 082 373 5950.
Eat: Le Rendez-Vous Restaurant, Crocworld, 039 976 0083.
Sleep: Blue Marlin Hotel, 180 Scott Street, 039 978 3361.

COST: Adults R65, children 4–12 R40, children under 4 free, pensioners R45; School tours are R30 per child, and tour groups of 20 individuals or more are R50 per person

---

2 Galleria Ice Rink
www.skategalleria.co.za

2/5 Party venue rating   5/5 Rainy day option

The ice rink at Galleria Shopping Centre is open every day, giving visitors the chance to hone their skills, try ice skating for the first time, or join in one of the clubs, such as ice hockey. There are two sessions every day, along with an evening session.

Tel number	031 904 1156
Address	Entertainment level, Galleria Shopping Centre, corner Moss Kolnik and Arbour roads, aManzimtoti
GPS marker	30°02'04"S; 30°53'57"E
Opening hours	Open daily; day sessions are 10am–1pm and 2pm–5pm, evening sessions are 7:30pm–10:30pm, and until 11pm Friday and Saturday
Most appropriate age group	6+
Pram/wheelchair-friendly	No
Baby-changing facility	Yes
Nearest hospital	Netcare Kingsway Hospital, 031 904 7000

Take note:
You can hire your skates from the ice rink. The smallest size skate available is a size 9. If children can fit into this size, then they are welcome. There are no baby-changing facilities at the rink, but these are available in the centre. Venue closed for reservations until November 2015.

Nearby

Play/do: Epic Karting, Galleria Shopping Centre, 031 904 5470. Fun Company, Galleria Shopping Centre, 031 904 5770.
Eat: John Dory's, Galleria Shopping Centre, 031 904 2489.
Shop: Galleria Shopping Centre, corner Moss Kolnik and Arbour roads, 031 904 2233.

COST: Entry is R40, skate hire R20; groups (including skate hire) of 10 or more pay R50 per person, 20 or more pay R45, and school groups R30 per learner; sharpening is R40 per pair of skates

---

3 Splash Waterworld
www.splashwaterworld.co.za

4/5 Party venue rating   0/5 Rainy day option

This beachside water park offers entertainment for the whole family. They have 10 water slides catering to different age groups, as well as a pool area and lazy river, along which you can drift in a tube. There are also heated pools and rides for smaller children. Or you can try your hand at mini golf. Visitors are allowed to take in their own refreshments, or purchase these at the venue, and a braai area is available. Costs are determined by whether or not a visitor is above or below a mark at the ticket office.

Tel number	031 904 2273
	082 781 5535
Address	97 Beach Road, aManzimtoti
GPS marker	30°02'56"S; 30°53'25"E
Opening hours	10am–5pm in summer, 6pm–9pm for summer Friday night riding, and 10am–4pm in winter
Most appropriate age group	3+
Pram/wheelchair-friendly	Yes
Baby-changing facility	No
Nearest hospital	Netcare Kingsway Hospital, 031 904 7000

Nearby
Visit/see: aManzimtoti Bird Sanctuary, uMdoni Road, 031 903 7498. The Book Boutique, 26 Rockview Road, 031 903 6692.
Play/do: Funland Entertainment, 19 Beach Road, 031 903 1068.
Eat: RJ's Steakhouse, 19 Beach Road, 031 903 8985.

COST Day pass (above 1.2m) R90, day pass (below 1.2m) R55; late pass after 2pm (above 1.2m) R55, late pass (below 1.2m) R40; a 10-day pass is R450; pensioners (with pension card) pay R25; umbrella and lounger hire R25 each, chair hire R15 each, locker hire R25 and boogie board hire R20 per hour, or R40 per day; Friday night riding (during summer school terms) R40; normal putt putt (without day pass) R10 per game

Inland

1. 1000 Hills Country Village
2. Africa Whispers
3. Giba Gorge MTB Park
4. Groovy Balls Adventure Park
5. Karkloof Canopy Tour
6. Lucky Bean
7. Makaranga Garden Lodge
8. Oxford Village
9. Phezulu Safari Park
10. Winsome View Animal Farm and Country Bistro

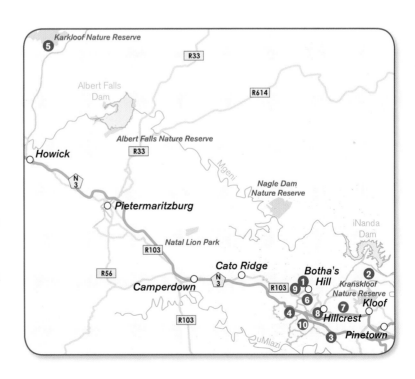

1 1000 Hills Country Village

www.facebook.com/1000hillscountryvillage

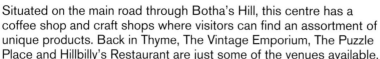

2/5 Party venue rating

3/5 Rainy day option

Situated on the main road through Botha's Hill, this centre has a coffee shop and craft shops where visitors can find an assortment of unique products. Back in Thyme, The Vintage Emporium, The Puzzle Place and Hillbilly's Restaurant are just some of the venues available.

Tel number	031 777 1788 (Hillbilly's Restaurant)
Address	168 Old Main Road, Botha's Hill
GPS marker	29°45'01"S; 30°43'52"E
Opening hours	9am–4:30pm daily
Most appropriate age group	6+
Pram/wheelchair-friendly	No
Baby-changing facility	No
Nearest hospital	Hillcrest Private Hospital, 031 768 8000

Nearby
Visit/see: Embocraft, 237 Old Main Road, 031 765 3697.
Eat: The Pot and Kettle, 168 Old Main Road, 031 777 1312. The View Pancake Café, 330 Old Main Road, 031 777 1629. Talloula, 61 Old Main Road, 031 777 1586.

Take note:
Parties can be held at Hillbilly's Restaurant. The village is a collection of independently owned businesses, so times may vary for individual shops or restaurants.

---

2 Africa Whispers

www.africawhispers.co.za

4/5 Party venue rating

1/5 Rainy day option

This child-friendly restaurant and party venue overlooks iNanda Dam. You can sit under umbrellas at tables on the grass, or on the undercover patio, while you enjoy breakfast, brunch or lunch. Pony rides and a jumping castle are available. There is also some self-catering accommodation.

COST On-site horse-riding lessons and outrides are R100 per hour; pony rides are free

Tel number	031 776 3075
	083 270 0003
Address	11 Ridgemont Road, Crestholme
GPS marker	29°43'22"S; 30°50'41"E
Opening hours	The Country Café: 8am–5pm Friday to Sunday and public holidays, and Friday and Saturday nights for bookings and private functions
Most appropriate age group	4–10
Pram/wheelchair-friendly	Yes
Baby-changing facility	Yes
Nearest hospital	Hillcrest Private Hospital, 031 768 8000
	Life The Crompton Hospital, 031 737 3000

Nearby
Do: Watercrest Mall, 141 iNanda Road, Waterfall, 031 765 5345.
Play/sleep: iNanda Dam, off Blessing Ninela Road, 031 766 9946.
Eat: Navaho Springs Spur, Watercrest Mall, 031 763 1377.
For parents: Crinkley Bottom Park, 167 iNanda Road, 082 681 8506.

---

3 Giba Gorge MTB Park
www.gibagorge.co.za

Off the beaten track, this MTB park caters for all types of riders. Little children can ride around the grass, while those with a bit more experience can take to the smaller ramps. A bigger track is perfect for those getting the hang of riding over ramps, and for serious BMXers, there is a challenging track. Hiking and MTB trails run from the parking lot and extend throughout the park and you can take a ride to a waterfall. For spectators, there is a coffee shop, or base yourself at one of the picnic tables, where there is a nearby jungle gym. A monthly market at the park also caters for the family.

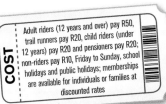

COST Adult riders (12 years and over) pay R50, trail runners pay R20, child riders (under 12 years) pay R20 and pensioners pay R20; non-riders pay R10, Friday to Sunday, school holidays and public holidays; memberships are available for individuals or families at discounted rates

Tel number	031 769 1527
Address	110 Stockville Road, Pinetown
GPS marker	29°49'38"S; 30°46'54"E
Opening hours	7am–5pm for non-members; members have 24-hour access
Most appropriate age group	5+
Pram/wheelchair-friendly	Yes
Baby-changing facility	No
Nearest hospital	Hillcrest Private Hospital, 031 768 8000
	Life The Crompton Hospital, 031 737 3000

Nearby
Visit/see: The Play Market, Giba Gorge MTB Park, 071 307 0823.
Play/do: Boot Camp Giba Valley, Stockville Road, 082 782 6432.
Giba Gorge Horse Trails, Stockville Road, 082 623 3783.

Take note:
The road to Giba Gorge is a dirt road, but it is in good condition. Hot showers are available. There is secure parking on site.

4 Groovy Balls Adventure Park

www.groovyballs.co.za

In zorbing, participants get inside a big ball, which then rolls down a hill. This is the only zorbing park in the region and the grooves, or courses, have been professionally designed. The park offers several different courses and types of balls to cater for everyone. They also offer paintball, target shooting and go-karting, all catering to a range of age groups. A tuck shop is available, or you can take a picnic or make use of the braai areas. There is a children's play area, and toilets, a shower and change rooms are provided.

Tel number	084 330 3112
Address	Lot 152, off Capital Hill Drive, Cliffdale
GPS marker	29°46'46"S; 30°42'03"E
Opening hours	8:30am–6pm Tuesday to Sunday; booking is essential
Most appropriate age group	4+
Pram/wheelchair-friendly	Yes
Baby-changing facility	No
Nearest hospital	Hillcrest Private Hospital (8.2km), 031 768 8000

Nearby
Visit/see: African Birds of Prey, Lion Park Road, Camperdown, 031 785 4382.
Play/do: Valley Ridge Farm, Killarney View Road, 079 883 6991.
For parents: Cato Ridge Golf Club, Chamberlain Lane, 031 782 1692.

COST: Aqua Ball 2 people per ride R150 per person; Harness Ball 2 people per ride R200 per person; Go Karting R15 per lap with a minimum of 5 laps; Target shooting 40 shots per person at R1 per shot

COST: 3 rounds Sumo Suit wrestling R150 per couple; 3 rounds Bumper balls R150 per couple; Paint Ball: Combat includes all gear and 100 shots at R110 per person

Take note: This venue is open for bookings only.

COST: Paint Ball: Full Metal Jacket includes all gear and 200 shots at R140 per person; Paint Ball: Hero includes all gear and 300 shots R185 per person; Paint Ball: Commando includes all gear and 500 shots R240 per person. Corporate and school packages also available.

5 Karkloof Canopy Tour
www.karkloofcanopytour.co.za

3/5 Party venue rating

0/5 Rainy day option

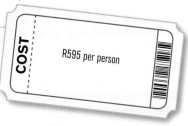

Karkloof Nature Reserve

Albert Falls Dam

Albert Falls Natu

Howick   R33

Based just outside Howick, and near the beautiful Karkloof Falls, these canopy tours let visitors glide through the trees on a series of zip lines. The indigenous forest at Karkloof is made up of a variety of trees and giant ferns and is home to magnificent birdlife, all of which you will see up close. There are nine platforms and eight zip lines, and the two-hour tour is generally suitable for those aged 7 and older. Professional guides are there to help you along, and to provide interesting details about your surroundings. Tours include a light lunch, once you are back on the ground.

COST

R595 per person

Tel number	033 330 3415
	076 241 2888
Address	Karkloof Road, Howick
GPS marker	29°19'23"S; 30°15'44"E
Opening hours	Time slots available
	8:30am–2pm daily
Most appropriate age group	7+
Pram/wheelchair-friendly	No
Baby-changing facility	No
Nearest hospital	Mediclinic Howick,
	033 330 2456

Take note:
Due to slides being long and fast, there is a weight restriction of 130kg. A short briefing DVD is shown to guests, so you will know what to expect. Parties are welcome but are not organised by the company; you need to arrange everything.

Nearby
Visit/see: Howick Falls, Howick, or Howick Museum, Fallsview, 033 239 9240.
Play/do: uMgeni Valley Nature Reserve, off the Karkloof Road, 033 330 3931.
Piggly Wiggly Country Village, 1 Dargle Road, 033 234 2911.
Eat: Yellowwood Café and Restaurant, 1 Shafton Road, 033 330 2461.
The Karkloof Farmers Market, Karkloof Road, 082 851 8649.

Special events
The Karkloof Classic MTB event takes place in May, and *The Witness* Hilton Arts Festival, held at Hilton College in September, includes plays, art and other festivities

---

6 Lucky Bean
www.luckybean.co

5/5 Party venue rating

3/5 Rainy day option

iNanda Dam

Ridge   Botha's Hill   Kranskloof Nature Reserve

R103   Kloof

Hillcrest

uMlazi   Pinetown

Well known for its excellent coffee, this playground for children also gives parents a chance to relax while their children work off steam in a secure area. The venue offers indoor and outdoor play areas. The undercover play barn has ball ponds, swings and a sandpit to keep children entertained. Outside, a bike track, swings and a jungle gym are welcome distractions, as are the playhouses that have an assortment of make-believe and dress-up goodies. Tables are dotted around the venue for parents who can order light meals and refreshments from the kitchen. Holiday activities are also frequently offered.

Tel number	082 216 3892
Address	10 Cadmoor Road, Assagay
GPS marker	29°45'57"S; 30°44'30"E
Opening hours	9am–4pm Tuesday to Sunday
Most appropriate age group	1–6
Pram/wheelchair-friendly	Yes
Baby-changing facility	Yes
Nearest hospital	Hillcrest Private Hospital, 031 768 8000

COST Adults free entry, children 0–6 R20

Nearby

Visit/see: Animal Farmyard, 3 Lello Road, 031 765 2240.

Eat: Chantecler Hotel, 27 Clement Stott Road, 031 765 2613. The Olive Garden, Bona Terra Road, 031 768 1314.

Shop: The Mushroom Farm, 450 Kassier Road, 031 768 2143. Shongweni Farmers Market (every Saturday), Alverston Road, 031 777 4686.

Take note: Lucky Bean is a no-smoking and zero-alcohol venue. Play areas are suitable for ages 0–6 years, but everyone is welcome. The tea garden is suitable for all ages. Plastic scooters are available for children to use.

---

(7) Makaranga Garden Lodge
www.makaranga.com

0/5 Party venue rating   **1/5** Rainy day option

Children can explore the gardens, swim in the pool or play on the jungle gym, while you enjoy a picnic on the grass or a bite to eat at Nonna, the restaurant. There is an inside area, or outside deck, or adults can choose to sit in the child-free area. Accommodation is also available.

Tel number	031 764 6616
Address	1A Igwababa Road, Kloof
GPS marker	29°47'32"S; 30°49'06"E
Opening hours	Restaurant: 6:30am–10pm Monday to Saturday, 6:30am–6pm Sunday; gardens and pool access close at 6pm
Most appropriate age group	5+
Pram/wheelchair-friendly	Yes
Baby-changing facility	Yes
Nearest hospital	Hillcrest Private Hospital, 031 768 8000 Life The Crompton Hospital, 031 737 3000

Take note: Children need to be supervised at all times, especially in the pool, and are not allowed to climb on the statues. Picnic blankets, baskets and umbrellas can be hired. Guests may not bring in their own picnic baskets. Golf carts are available for hire for the mobility impaired.

Nearby

Visit/see: Krantzkloof Nature Reserve,152 Kloof Falls Road.
Play/do: Adventure Golf, 10 Msenga Road, 031 764 6694.
Kloof SPCA, 29 Village Road, 031 764 1212.
Eat: Bellevue Café, 5 Bellevue Road, 031 717 2780. Piggly
Wiggly, 10 Msenga Road, 031 764 2497. Bella and Boo
frozen yoghurt bar, Maytime Centre, 20 Charles Way,
031 764 2092.

COST Free entry to the restaurants and hotel. R60 per car for those just visiting the gardens.

---

8 Oxford Village
www.facebook.com/oxfordvillagehillcrest

 4/5 Party venue rating
 3/5 Rainy day option

This centre boasts a number of family-orientated shops and food
outlets, as well as various venues that cater for children. These include
a five-a-side soccer pitch and Pallet Jacks, a pay playground and family
restaurant. Pallet Jacks also do children's parties. The Mozart Ice Cream
Factory and Candy Land are also geared towards the children. For parents, there are
a number of restaurants and a food outlets, and you can get plenty of shopping done
at the same time, with the Oxford Freshmarket, a Build It, and many boutique stores at
the complex. There is accessible parking throughout the centre.

Tel number	031 765 2500
Address	9 Old Main Road, Hillcrest
GPS marker	29°47'20"S; 30°46'26"E
Opening hours	Open daily; Oxford Freshmarket: 7am–7:30pm daily; shop and restaurant times vary
Most appropriate age group	5+
Pram/wheelchair-friendly	Yes
Baby-changing facility	Yes, at Pallet Jacks
Nearest hospital	Hillcrest Private Hospital, 031 768 8000

Nearby

Visit/see: Springside Nature Reserve, Springside Road,
031 765 6809. Hillcrest Aids Centre, 26 Old Main
Road, 031 765 5866.
Eat: Oscars Café Hillcrest, Lillies Quarter, 12 Old Main
Road, 031 765 7322. Primi Piatti, Richdens Village
Centre, 59 Old Main Road, 031 765 6920.
Shop: Keachea, Oxford Village, 031 765 2354.
For parents: Stretta Café,
The Colony Centre,
50 Old Main Road,
031 765 8862.

Take note:
The centre is situated
on a hill, so while there
are ramps and paths
throughout, these can
be steep in places.

9 Phezulu Safari Park
www.phezulusafaripark.co.za

4/5
Party venue rating

1/5
Rainy day option

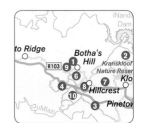

The park offers an authentic Zulu experience, with the Boma, a Zulu-themed restaurant, traditional Zulu dancing and a tour through the Zulu village. There is also a crocodile and snake park where visitors can see old and young crocodiles and venomous snakes. A play area, tearoom and café are available nearby. Game drives are also on offer, giving visitors the chance to see wildebeest, impala, blesbok, zebra and giraffe, while learning about medicinal plants in the area. An assortment of traditional African crafts are on offer at the gift shop.

Tel number	031 777 1000
Address	Old Main Road, Botha's Hill
GPS marker	29°45'14"S; 30°43'24"E
Opening hours	Zulu dancing shows are at 10am, 11:30am, 2pm and 3:30pm; shows last 30 minutes, followed by the village tour lasting 15–20 minutes; game drives take place every hour 9am–4pm; Boma Restaurant: 8am–4:30pm Wednesday to Sunday; Spaza Restaurant: 8am–4:30pm daily
Most appropriate age group	5+
Pram/wheelchair-friendly	No
Baby-changing facility	No
Nearest hospital	Hillcrest Private Hospital, 031 768 8000

Nearby

Visit/see: The Inchanga Choo Choo, departs from Kloof Station, Old Main Road, Kloof, 087 808 7715.
Play/do: Hillcrest Paintball, 23 Wootton Avenue, 074 172 1309.
Eat: Intaba View, 10 Old Main Road, 031 783 4011. The 1000 Hills Chef School (booking essential), 2 Wootton Avenue, 031 777 1566.

Special event

The Comrades Marathon sees runners coming through on Old Main Road every year in late May or early June

COST The Combo package includes the village tour, Zulu dancing show, crocodile and snake park tour: adults R150, children under 12 R100; village tour and Zulu dancing: adults R110, children under 12 R70; crocodile and snake park hourly tours: adults R50, children under 12 R40; game drive: adults R225, children under 12 R125

Take note:
Entrance to the park is free, which gives visitors access to the restaurants and curio shops. Tickets to the tours and game drive need to be purchased.

10 Winsome View Animal Farm and Country Bistro

5/5 Party venue rating

1/5 Rainy day option

www.winsomeview.co.za

Children can interact with and learn about the animals on this farm, while also enjoying activities like playing on the jungle gyms and in the sandpit or riding a pony. Children can 'adopt' an animal on the farm. The Country Bistro offers breakfasts, light meals and refreshments.

Tel number	031 769 1500
	082 892 1615
Address	D71B Hawkstone Road, Summerveld, Hillcrest
GPS marker	29°47'56"S; 30°43'07"E
Opening hours	9am–3pm Tuesday to Sunday and public holidays
Most appropriate age group	3–10
Pram/wheelchair-friendly	Yes
Baby-changing facility	Yes
Nearest hospital	Hillcrest Private Hospital, 031 768 8000

Nearby

Visit/see: The Shongweni Dam, 43 Old Main Road, Hillcrest, 031 769 1283. Andrew Walford's Pottery, B9 Zig Zag Farm, 031 769 1363.
Play/do: Spirit of Adventure, based at Shongweni Dam, 0861 333 919.
Eat: Summerveld Country Lodge, Hawkstone Road, 031 769 1594.

Take note: In poor weather, there is undercover seating in the bistro. Wheelchairs and prams can go most places, but not everywhere.

COST R20 entry, specials are available for parties and school tours; pony rides are R8, feed bags are R7, or buy all three of these for R32

Getting around Johannesburg

Joburg is best navigated by car due to the public transport system not servicing all the areas and it can also be unreliable. There are numerous rental car companies to choose from as well as metered taxis. In the areas where public transport is an option, you have access to the Gautrain rail network and connecting Gautrain Bus service, the hop-on, hop-off City Sightseeing red bus and the Rea Vaya Bus Rapid Transit System.

The Gautrain connects OR Tambo International Airport with Rhodesfield, Marlboro, Sandton, Rosebank and Park stations. It also heads north, stopping at Midrand, Centurion, Pretoria and Hatfield. The City Sightseeing red bus offers a circular route that departs and ends at Park Station and visits 11 major tourist sites around central Joburg. Rea Vaya currently only operates in the central suburbs, connecting the CBD, Newtown, Braamfontein, Parktown and Auckland Park, and also offers a circular inner city route.

Rental car companies

Europcar
24-hour call centre 0861 131 000 or
011 479 4000
info@europcar.co.za
www.europcar.co.za

Avis
0861 021 111
www.avis.co.za

Bidvest Car Rental
0861 017 722
reservations@bidvestcarrental.co.za
www.bidvestcarrental.co.za

Metered taxis

Uber
www.uber.com

Snappcab
www.snappcab.com

Gautrain
0800 428 87246
Gautrain Bus 010 223 1098
www.gautrain.co.za

Rea Vaya
0860 JOBURG (562874)
www.reavaya.org.za

Johannesburg City Centre and East

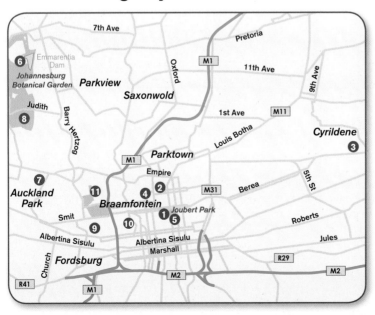

1. City Sightseeing red bus
2. Constitution Hill
3. Derrick Avenue
4. Joburg Theatre
5. Johannesburg Art Gallery (JAG)
6. Johannesburg Botanical Garden – Emmarentia Dam
7. Lindfield Victorian House Museum
8. Melville Koppies
9. Oriental Plaza
10. The Sci-Bono Discovery Centre
11. University of the Witwatersrand

1 City Sightseeing red bus
www.citysightseeing.co.za

2/5
Party venue rating

5/5
Rainy day option

Tour central Joburg aboard a double-decker bus that stops at sites around the city. They operate on a hop-on, hop-off basis so you can view the city at your leisure. Buses depart from the first stop, Park Station, every 40 minutes and conduct a circular route of the city, which takes about 90 minutes. The sites en route include Gandhi Square, Carlton Centre, the James Hall Transport Museum, the Apartheid Museum and Gold Reef City, the Mining District, Newtown Precinct, Wits University, Braamfontein and Constitution Hill. You are able to buy tickets at the ticket offices in Park Station and at Gold Reef City, on the bus using a debit or credit card, or online. An audio guide is included in the ticket price, with commentary in 15 languages and also a children's channel.

Take note: You are able to combine your Joburg sightseeing trip with a tour of Soweto.

Tel number	0861 RED BUS (733 287)
Address	First departure point: Gautrain Park Station, Wolmarans Street, between Rissik and Joubert streets, Braamfontein (secure parking at the station)
GPS marker	26°11'42"S; 28°02'30"E
Opening Hours	9am–5:55pm daily
Closest public transport	Gautrain Park Station (one minute)
Most appropriate age group	1+
Pram/wheelchair-friendly	Yes
Baby-changing facility	No
Nearest hospital	Netcare Park Lane Hospital, 011 480 4000

COST: One-day pass: adults R150, children 5–17 years R80, children under 5 years free; one-day pass combined with a Soweto tour: adults R370, children 5–17 years R200, children under 5 years free

2 Constitution Hill
www.constitutionhill.org.za

0/5
Party venue rating

3/5
Rainy day option

This National Heritage Site was built in 1892 to function as a prison, except for the brief period of the South African War (1899–1902) when it was a military defence post. It was a transitory prison where prisoners were held until they were sentenced and transferred to serve their prison terms elsewhere. Some of the most notable prisoners were Mahatma Gandhi and Nelson Mandela. In the mid-1990s, the site was chosen for the new Constitutional Court, which is the highest court in the country on constitutional matters. The centre offers guided tours and temporary exhibitions as well as a full programme of educational activities.

Tel number	011 381 3100
Address	1 Kotze Street
GPS marker	26°11'25"S; 28°02'31"E
Closest public transport	Park Station Gautrain (four minutes); take the J1 Gautrain Bus or the inner city route on the Rea Vaya; bus stop on Joubert Street City Sightseeing red bus (stop 12)
Opening hours	9am–4pm Monday, Tuesday, Thursday, Friday, 9am–1pm Wednesday, 10am–2pm Saturday and Sunday
Most appropriate age group	11+
Pram/wheelchair-friendly	Yes
Baby-changing facility	Yes
Nearest hospital	Netcare Park Lane Hospital, 011 480 4000

COST
Adults R50, pensioners R25, children R20, children under 5 years free

Take note:
Guided tours take place every hour, on the hour. Arrive 15 minutes beforehand to view a short background film.

 **Derrick Avenue**
www.gauteng.net

0/5 Party venue rating
2/5 Rainy day option

Two impressive archways mark the entrances to Derrick Avenue and let visitors know that they have entered Chinatown. The community is made up of Chinese and Taiwanese immigrants who arrived in Joburg in the 70s and 80s. Chinese supermarkets, karaoke bars and restaurants line the streets. The signage is in Mandarin, and very little English is spoken.

Tel number	011 085 2500
Address	Derrick Avenue, Cyrildene
GPS marker	26°10'43"S; 28°06'00"E
Opening hours	Times vary
Most appropriate age group	4+
Pram/wheelchair-friendly	Yes
Baby-changing facility	No
Nearest hospital	Netcare Linksfield Hospital, 011 647 3400

Take note:
Take your own wine to dinner.

Nearby
Eat: Shun Deck Chinese Restaurant, 30 Derrick Avenue, 011 025 2979.
Shop: Bruma Oriental City, 86 Marcia Street, Bruma, 011 615 4802. Eastgate Shopping Centre, 43 Bradford Road, 011 479 6000.

Special event

Chinese New Year celebrations are held in late January or early February

COST — Food costs vary

---

4 # Joburg Theatre
www.joburgtheatre.com

3/5 Party venue rating

5/5 Rainy day option

The theatre plays host to numerous local and international theatrical performances, including a pantomime over the festive period. The theatre complex is home to the People's Theatre, which stages children's productions throughout the year, and the Joburg Ballet whose permanent and ad-hoc dancers, skilled in both classical ballet and contemporary dance, perform an extensive repertoire during their two seasons. You can take a sneak peek behind the curtains on a prebooked theatre tour that reveals the technically advanced stage and sheds light onto the superstitions behind each theatre performance.

COST — Varies per show; theatre tour: R25 per person (minimum 10 people, maximum 30 people)

Take note:
There is no ATM, so take cash if you want to buy sweets and snacks.

Tel number	011 877 6800, 0861 670 670
Address	Corner Hoofd and Loveday streets, Braamfontein
GPS marker	26°11'30"S; 28°02'17"E
Closest public transport	Park Station Gautrain (four minutes); take the J1 Gautrain Bus or the inner city route on the Rea Vaya; bus stop on Loveday Street
Opening hours	Vary per show; theatre tours: 9:30am and 3pm Monday to Friday, excluding public holidays (bookings essential)
Most appropriate age group	4+
Pram/wheelchair-friendly	Yes
Baby-changing facility	Yes (People's Theatre)
Nearest hospital	Netcare Park Lane Hospital, 011 480 4000

Nearby
Shop: Neighbourgoods Market, 73 Juta Street, 011 403 0413.

5 Johannesburg Art Gallery (JAG)

www.joburg.org.za

0/5 Party venue rating

5/5 Rainy day option

JAG has an immense collection of historical and contemporary art-works by local and international artists, including 17th-century Dutch paintings, 18th- and 19th-century British and European art, and 19th-century South African works. One can also view the traditional Brenthurst Collection of African pieces and the Jacques collection of headrests. The building was designed by British architect Edwin Lutyens and consists of 15 exhibition halls and sculpture gardens. Guided tours are available by prior arrangement.

Take note: There is secure parking at the gallery.

Tel number	011 725 3130
Address	Klein Street, Joubert Park
GPS marker	26°11'49"S; 28°02'50"E
Closest public transport	Gautrain Park Station (six minutes); take the inner city route on the Rea Vaya; bus stop on Twist Street
Opening hours	10am–5pm Tuesday to Sunday
Most appropriate age group	8+
Pram/wheelchair-friendly	Yes
Baby-changing facility	No
Nearest hospital	Netcare Park Lane Hospital, 011 480 4000

Nearby

Visit/see: Carlton Centre, while on a tour with Main Street Walks, 072 880 9583. Standard Bank Art Gallery, corner Simmonds and Frederick streets, 011 631 4467.
Play/do: Train trips to Magaliesburg (departing from Park Station) and Irene (departing from Rhodesfield) with Reefsteamers, 011 875 2354.
Eat/shop: Maboneng Precinct, 286 Fox Street, 011 592 0515.

6 Johannesburg Botanical Garden – Emmarentia Dam

www.jhbcityparks.com

4/5 Party venue rating

1/5 Rainy day option

Forming part of Joburg's green lung, the 81ha expanse is frequented by runners, picnickers and dog walkers. The gardens overlook Emma-rentia Dam, which is utilised by canoeists, boaters and a multitude of ducks and geese. Dogs are allowed in the southern part of the park, while the east side of the garden contains the rose and herb gardens and the main arboretum. The park is fenced and there are security guards at each entrance.

Take note: The park is at its greenest from November to April.

Tel number	011 712 6600
Address	Main entrance off Olifants Road, Emmarentia
GPS marker	26°09'25"S; 28°00'09"E
Opening hours	Sunrise to sunset
Most appropriate age group	1+
Pram/wheelchair-friendly	Yes
Baby-changing facility	No
Nearest hospital	Netcare Rosebank Hospital, 011 328 0500

Nearby

Play/do: Kinderspiel, 39A Greenhill Road, Emmarentia, 011 646 0870.

Eat: Dukes Burgers, 14 Gleneagles Road, Greenside, 011 486 0824.

Shop: Jozi Food Market, Pirates Sports Club, 25 Braeside Street, Greenside, 083 532 2992.
Fresh Earth Food Store, 103 Komatie Road, Emmarentia, 011 646 4404.

For parents: Cube Tasting Kitchen, 17 4th Avenue, Parktown North, 082 422 8158.

---

7 Lindfield Victorian House Museum

0/5 Party venue rating   *5/5* Rainy day option

www.lindfield.wix.com/museum

Step back in time in an authentic house museum overflowing with Victorian treasures. Tours of the house are led by Katharine Love, who currently resides in the museum and has done so since 1967. Katharine dresses in a parlourmaid's outfit and relates the history behind every room and tells stories about Victorian customs and way of life. The tour is followed by tea and refreshments.

Take note:
You are allowed to take photos in the museum as long as they are for noncommercial use.

Tel number	011 726 2932
Address	72 Richmond Avenue, Auckland Park
GPS marker	26°11'07"S; 28°00'29"E
Opening hours	Open by appointment only
Most appropriate age group	7+
Pram/wheelchair-friendly	Yes
Baby-changing facility	No
Nearest hospital	Netcare Milpark Hospital, 011 480 5600

COST R50 per person, or, with tea and cake, adults R70, pensioners and children R50; high tea R120 per person

Nearby
Visit/see: Melville Koppies, park at Marks Park, Judith Road, Emmarentia, 011 482 4797.

8 Melville Koppies
www.mk.org.za

 0/5 Party venue rating
 0/5 Rainy day option

At this nature reserve and Joburg City Heritage Site, remnants from the Stone Age and Iron Age can be found, such as stone tools and an iron-smelting furnace, which was excavated in 1963. The indigenous vegetation of the Koppies is an example of the Highveld's rich diversity in trees, grasses and flowers. The central part of the reserve has controlled access only for people on organised tours and hikes, which take place regularly. The eastern and western parts of the park are open daily and socialised dogs on leads are welcome.

COST Guided hikes from R50 per adult and R20 per child

Tel number	011 482 4797
Address	Park at Marks Park, Judith Road, Emmarentia
GPS marker	26°10'00"S; 28°00'16"E
Opening hours	Sunrise to sunset, guided hikes at 8am, 8:30am or 3pm most Saturdays
Most appropriate age group	6+
Pram/wheelchair-friendly	No
Baby-changing facility	No
Nearest hospital	Medicross Meldene, 011 482 2291, 011 727 3404

Take note:
It is advisable not to walk in the western part of the park, and when you walk in the eastern part to do so in a group

Nearby
<u>Visit/see</u>: Lindfield Victorian House Museum, 72 Richmond Avenue, Auckland Park, 011 726 2932.
<u>Eat</u>: Bambanani Mediterranean Restaurant, 85 4th Avenue, 011 482 2900.
<u>Shop</u>: Bamboo Lifestyle Centre, corner Rustenburg Road and Ninth Street, 011 726 1701, 083 284 6226.
<u>For parents</u>: Melville Wellness Centre and Day Spa, 37 Arundel Road, 011 477 5866.

9 Oriental Plaza
www.orientalplaza.co.za

 0/5 Party venue rating
 3/5 Rainy day option

The Plaza is Joburg's 'Little India' and a great spot for an eclectic and vibrant shopping experience. With over 360 stores, you are sure to find bargains on exotic and local fabric, clothing, curtains, bedding, shoes, jewellery, kitchenware and lots more. The Plaza was established in the 70s after traders were forced to vacate the city centre under the apartheid government's Group Areas Act. The traders who could afford it purchased retail space at the new centre and, without the burden of monthly rentals, were able to offer their products at discounted prices.

Take note:
Selected stores are closed between 12pm and 2pm on Fridays.

Tel number	011 838 6752
Address	60 Lilian Ngoyi Street, Fordsburg
GPS marker	26°12'09"S; 28°01'26"E
Opening hours	9am–5pm Monday to Friday, 9am–3pm Saturday
Most appropriate age group	5+
Pram/wheelchair-friendly	Yes
Baby-changing facility	No
Nearest hospital	Netcare Garden City, 011 495 5000
	Netcare Milpark Hospital, 011 480 5600

Nearby
Visit/see: Bag Factory Artists' Studios,
10 Mahlathini Street, 011 834 9181.
Eat: Indian Coffee Shop, 48 Central Road,
011 492 2089.

---

10 The Sci-Bono Discovery Centre
www.sci-bono.co.za

The Sci-Bono Discovery Centre is a science museum with over 350 interactive exhibits appealing to children and adults alike. The centre is housed in the historic Electric Workshop in Newtown, the first President Street power station, commissioned in 1906 to power the electric tram system. The power station operated until March 1907 when there was an explosion in the boiler house. Sci-Bono holds numerous exhibitions, talks and holiday programmes during the year, and the facilities include a career resource library where they offer comprehensive career guidance and support to all Gauteng schools. There is a coffee shop serving light meals and snacks.

Take note:
There isn't an ATM, but they do have card facilities. There is secure parking.

Tel number	011 639 8400
Address	Corner Miriam Makeba and President streets, Newtown
GPS marker	26°12'16"S; 28°01'59"E
Closest public transport	Park Station Gautrain (five minutes); City Sightseeing red bus (stop 9)
Opening hours	9am–5pm Monday to Friday, 9:30am–4:30pm Saturday and Sunday
Most appropriate age group	5+
Pram/wheelchair-friendly	Yes
Baby-changing facility	Yes
Nearest hospital	Netcare Park Lane Hospital, 011 480 4000

COST
Adults and teenagers 17 years and older R40, pensioners and students R25, children 3–16 years R25, children under 3 years free

Nearby

Visit/see: MuseuMAfricA, 121 Lilian Ngoyi Street, 011 833 5624. Market Theatre, corner Lilian Ngoyi and Miriam Makeba streets, 011 832 1641/2/3.
Shop: Newtown Junction Shopping Centre, corner Miriam Makeba and Carr streets, 011 492 0105.
For parents: SAB World of Beer, 15 Helen Joseph Street, 011 836 4900 ext. 115.

 11

University of the Witwatersrand
www.wits.ac.za

5/5 Party venue rating

5/5 Rainy day option

Wits University began as the South African School of Mines in Kimberley in 1896. It was later moved to Joburg, where it became the University of the Witwatersrand in 1922 and adopted a policy of nondiscrimination on race or any other grounds. Within the confines of the university one is able to learn more about the stars and planets at the Planetarium, learn about the history of humankind and view rock art at the Origins Centre, or appreciate contemporary art at the Wits Art Museum.

Take note: The Planetarium, Origins Centre and Wits Art Museum all hold regular talks, shows and exhibitions.

Tel number	Planetarium: 011 717 1390
	Origins Centre: 011 717 4700
	Wits Art Museum: 011 717 1365 (Monday to Friday),
	011 717 1358 (Saturday and Sunday)
Address	Off Empire Road, Milner Park
GPS marker	26°11'19"S; 28°01'41"E (Planetarium)
	26°11'34"S; 28°01'45"E (Origins Centre)
	26°11'34"S; 28°02'07"E (Wits Art Museum)
Closest public transport	Park Station Gautrain (5 minutes); take the inner city route on the Rea Vaya, bus stop corner Jorissen and Eendracht streets; City Sightseeing red bus (stop 10)
Opening hours	Planetarium: show times vary, show for 5–8-year-olds 10:30am most Saturdays, book in advance; Origins Centre: 10am–5pm Monday to Sunday, starts closing 4:45pm; Wits Art Museum: 10am–4pm Wednesday to Sunday
Most appropriate age group	6+
Pram/wheelchair friendly	Yes
Baby changing facility	No
Nearest hospital	Netcare Milpark Hospital, 011 480 5600

Nearby

Visit/see: Linder Auditorium, 27 St Andrews Road, Parktown, 011 717 3223/3007.
Play/do: Cycology Electric Bicycle Tours, 44 Stanley Avenue, Milpark, 073 383 7621.
Eat: Olives and Plates Restaurant, Wits Club and Conference Centre, Yale Road, off Empire Road, Parktown, 011 717 9365. Several cafés at 44 Stanley Ave, Milpark, 011 482 4444.

COST Free entry; Planetarium: adults R40, pensioners, students and children R27, family ticket (two adults, their children and grandparents) R150; Origins Centre: adults R80, pensioners R65, children under 12 years R40, includes audio guides available in isiZulu, seSotho, English, Afrikaans, French and German; Wits Art Museum: free entry

South of Johannesburg

1. Gold Reef City
2. James Hall Museum of Transport
3. Mandela House
4. Rietvlei Zoo Farm

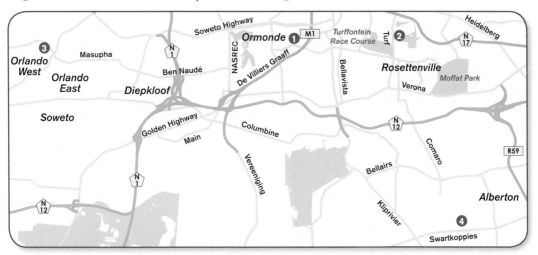

1 Gold Reef City
www.goldreefcity.co.za

5/5 Party venue rating

1/5 Rainy day option

Gold Reef City is an amusement park themed around the gold rush that started in 1886, with buildings to match the period, staff dressed in period costumes and a gold heritage tour that descends into the bowels of the earth for a tour of an underground mine. The theme park rides are for thrill-seekers of all ages, ranging from the terrifying Miner's revenge and Tower of Terror with a fear-factor rating of eight and 10 respectively, to the Cups & Saucers, bumper cars and Ferris wheel, which are suitable for all ages. There is also a 4-D theatre with hydraulic seats, a range of smells and 3-D visuals, and several restaurants and fast-food outlets dotted around the park that cater to all tastes.

COST: Thrill rider R175, Major rider R135, non-rider R100, R110 per person under 1.3m, pensioner Thrill rider R150, pensioner Major rider R115, students R150, family ticket (two adults and two children under 16 years) R550, children under 3 years free; Jozi's Story of Gold: R265, children under 1.3m R200, children under 6 years are not permitted

Take note:
Get there early to avoid the long queues. You are not allowed to take your own food or drinks into the park.

Tel number	011 248 6800
Address	Corner Northern Parkway and Data Crescent, Ormonde
GPS marker	26°14'15"S; 28°00'48"E
Closest public transport	Park Station Gautrain (20 minutes); City Sightseeing red bus (stop 6)
Opening hours	9:30am–5pm Wednesday to Sunday, open daily during Gauteng public school holidays; Jozi's Story of Gold Heritage: daily at 9am, 10am, 11am, 2pm and 3pm
Most appropriate age group	6+
Pram/wheelchair-friendly	Yes
Baby-changing facility	Yes
Nearest hospital	Netcare Mulbarton Hospital, 011 682 4300

Nearby
Visit/see: Apartheid Museum, Northern Parkway and Gold Reef Road, 011 309 4700. The Lyric Theatre, corner Northern Parkway and Data Crescent, 011 248 5168/5229.
Sleep: Gold Reef City Theme Park Hotel, Shaft 14, Northern Parkway, 011 248 5700.
For parents: Gold Reef City Casino, corner Northern Parkway and Data Crescent, 011 248 5000.

---

2 James Hall Museum of Transport
www.jhmt.org.za

2/5 Party venue rating
5/5 Rainy day option

The James Hall Museum of Transport is the largest and most comprehensive museum of land transport in South Africa. Visitors can glimpse a fascinating collection of memorabilia, artefacts and special-interest vehicles as well as an extremely rare and exciting collection of steam vehicles. The collection includes animal-drawn carts, horse-drawn trams, ox-wagons, bicycles (including penny-farthings), electric cars, rickshaws and other self-propelled vehicles. The oldest motor car on display is a 1900 Clement Panhard. Tours are available by prior arrangement.

Take note:
Take along a picnic to enjoy in Pioneer Park, which surrounds a lake called Wemmer Pan. On selected evenings in the year the musical fountains perform a spectacular light and sound show. Dates posted on the Joburg City Parks website.

Tel number	011 435 9718, 011 435 9485/6/7
Address	Pioneer Park, Rosettenville Road, La Rochelle
GPS marker	26°14'02"S; 28°03'13"E
Closest public transport	Park Station Gautrain (13 minutes); City Sightseeing red bus (stop 5)
Opening hours	9am–5pm Tuesday to Friday, 9am–5pm (closed 12pm–1pm) Saturday and Sunday
Most appropriate age group	4+
Pram/wheelchair-friendly	Yes
Baby-changing facility	No
Nearest hospital	Netcare Mulbarton Hospital, 011 682 4300

Nearby
Play/do: Gold Reef City Theme Park, corner Northern Parkway and Data Crescent, Ormonde, 011 248 6800.

0/5
Party venue rating

5/5
Rainy day option

③ Mandela House
www.mandelahouse.co.za

Vilakazi Street is the only street in the world that was home to two Nobel Peace Laureates, Nelson Mandela and Archbishop Emeritus Desmond Tutu. Mandela House has been turned into a museum to preserve the history, heritage and legacy of the Mandela family. Nelson Mandela lived there from 1946 to 1962, and then again for 11 days when he was released from prison in 1990. The humble house, still bearing the marks from attacks involving petrol bombs, has some original furnishings and memorabilia. The museum allows 20 visitors in at a time for ease of access. At the corner of Vilakazi and Khumalo streets you can see an artwork of eight man-sized hands spelling 'Vilakazi' in sign language.

Tel number	011 936 7754
Address	8115 Vilakazi Street, Orlando West, Soweto
GPS marker	26°14'19"S; 27°54'31"E
Closest public transport	City Sightseeing red bus, Soweto Extension
Opening hours	9am–4:45pm daily; closed on Good Friday and Christmas Day
Most appropriate age group	8+
Pram/wheelchair-friendly	Yes
Baby-changing facility	No
Nearest hospital	Life Flora Clinic, 011 470 7777

Nearby

Visit/see: Hector Pieterson Museum and Memorial, Maseko Street, Orlando West, 011 536 0611.
Play/do: Orlando Towers Vertical Adventure Centre, corner Dynamo Street and Chris Hani Road, Orlando East, 071 674 4343.
Eat: Chaf Pozi, corner Nicholas and Kingsley Sithole streets, Orlando, 011 463 8895.
Shop: Maponya Mall, 2127 Chris Hani Road, Klipspruit, 011 938 4448.

COST Adults R60, students and children over 6 years R20, children under 6 years R5

Take note: It is best to visit Soweto with a tour operator.

4 Rietvlei Zoo Farm

www.rietvleilifestylecentre.co.za

Rietvlei Zoo Farm is a tranquil farm surrounded by natural wetlands, large trees and beautiful gardens. You can take along your camping chairs, umbrellas and picnic blankets for a picnic on the lawns and take advantage of their wide range of activities. You can feed the farm-yard animals, visit the aviary, ride the steam train and tractor cart, and explore the many mountain-biking and hiking trails.

Tel number	011 024 1512/4, 079 041 1488
Address	Swartkoppies Road, Alberton
GPS marker	26°18'44"S; 28°04'47"E
Opening hours	9am–5pm daily; for those with trail access cards, the hiking and cycling trails are open from 5am–7pm daily
Most appropriate age group	4+
Pram/wheelchair-friendly	Yes
Baby-changing facility	Yes
Nearest hospital	Netcare Mulbarton Hospital, 011 682 4300

Nearby

Visit/see: Thaba Eco Hotel and day spa, Impala Road, Klipriviersberg Nature Reserve, Kibler Park, 011 959 0777.

Play/do: Jungle Rumble, Panorama Shopping Centre, Kliprivier Road and Jordi Street, Mulbarton, 011 432 0403.

Shop: The Glen Shopping Centre, corner Orpen and Letaba streets, Oakdene, 011 435 9252.

COST — Picnic/braai area: adults and children 13 years and older R30, pensioners R10, children 2–12 years R20, children under 2 years free; R40 per vehicle, or you can park your vehicle at the entrance parking at no charge

COST — Zip line: single ride R150, family ticket (two adults and two children under 12 years) R800, includes a T-shirt, light meal and bottle of water; veggie packs to feed the farm animals R10 each

COST — Activities: pony rides R10, putt putt R10, steam train rides R20, tractor cart rides R10; trail access cards (walk, run, hike) R10 per entry, R100 for 10 entries; cycling R25 per ride per cyclist

Take note: They hire out braais and gazebos.

East Rand

1. AECI Dynamite Company Museum
2. Modderfontein Nature Reserve
3. Uncle Tim's Centre
4. Wild Waters

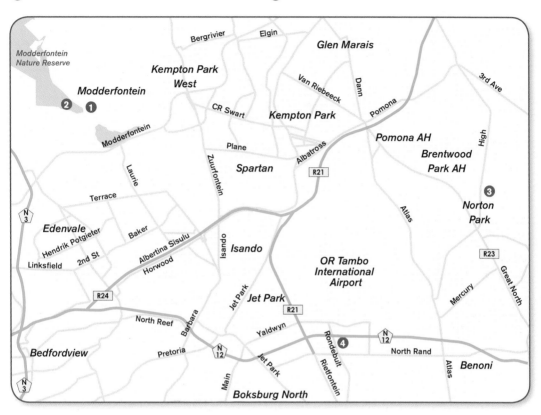

---

1 AECI Dynamite Company Museum

www.ekurhuleni.gov.za

0/5 Party venue rating

2/5 Rainy day option

In 1894, the Modderfontein Dynamite Factory was established to meet the needs of the growing gold-mining industry. The factory was constructed under the supervision of Franz Hoenig, seconded from the Nobel explosives factory at Pressburg, Hungary. For several decades, starting in the 1940s, South Africa was the largest producer of dynamite in the world. Find out more about the constructive and destructive uses for dynamite, how it is made and its purpose in the mining industry during your visit.

Tel number	011 608 2747
Address	2 Main Street, Modderfontein
GPS marker	26°04'32"S; 28°05'18"E
Opening hours	8am–12pm Monday to Friday
Most appropriate age group	12+
Pram/wheelchair-friendly	Yes
Baby-changing facility	No
Nearest hospital	Mediclinic Morningside, 011 282 5000
	Netcare Sunninghill Hospital, 011 806 1672

Nearby

Visit/see: Hunyani Snake City, 17 Voortrekker Avenue, Edenvale, 011 453 3257.

Play/do: Galaxy World, The Bedford Centre, corner Smith and Bradford roads, Bedfordview, 011 615 6877, 076 814 2827.

Shop/play: Stoneridge Centre, 1 Stoneridge Drive, Greenstone Park, Edenvale, 087 550 0237, 011 452 5721.

Eat: Val Bonne Country Estate, Arden Road, Modderfontein, 084 460 8564.

For parents: Oakes Brew House Modderfontein, 33 High Street, 011 458 6018, 083 260 7960.

---

2 Modderfontein Nature Reserve

www.modderfonteinreserve.co.za
www.centralparktrails.co.za

Party venue rating 4/5
Rainy day option 0/5

Modderfontein Nature Reserve

Modderfontein

The Modderfontein Nature Reserve is a 275ha private open space that is accessible to the public, but in a controlled fashion. The reserve is managed by the Endangered Wildlife Trust, which ensures the protection of indigenous flora and fauna and keeps the park in a pristine condition. There are mountain-biking and walking trails, and guided walks take place regularly.

Take note:
Dogs aren't allowed in the reserve.

Tel number	079 519 1589, 011 608 3535
Address	Arden Road (off Ardeer Road), Modderfontein
GPS marker	26°05'40"S; 28°09'14"E
Opening hours	6am–6pm daily; Central Park MTB trails: 6am–6pm Monday to Sunday, 6am–10pm Wednesday
Most appropriate age group	6+
Pram/wheelchair-friendly	No
Baby-changing facility	Yes (Val Bonne Country Estate)
Nearest hospital	Mediclinic Morningside, 011 282 5000

COST: Adults R30, children R15; Central Park MTB trails R50 per entry

Nearby

Eat: Val Bonne Country Estate, Arden Road, Modderfontein, 084 460 8564. Malagueta Mediterranean Restaurant, 2 Main Road, Eastleigh, 011 609 4910, 011 609 2793. Takis and Takis Greek Taverna Happyland, 7 Civin Drive, Senderwood, 011 027 3030, 076 324 6958. De Backery and De Molen, 47 Van Riebeeck Avenue, Edenvale, 011 453 2233/2222/8174.
Play/do: Pottery Junxion, 5 Glendower Place, 99 Linksfield Road, Dowerglen, Edenvale, 011 453 2721.
Shop/play: Hamleys toy store, Jimmy Jungles indoor play centre and Rush Indoor Trampoline Park, Greenstone Shopping Centre, 10 Stoneridge Drive, Edenvale, 011 524 0445.
Shop: Greenstone Shopping Centre, 10 Stoneridge Drive, Edenvale, 011 524 0445.

---

3 # Uncle Tim's Centre
www.uncletimscentre.co.za

Go antique shopping at Uncle Tim's Centre, a little Victorian shopping centre with a quaint collection of shops selling antiques and organic produce, children's teddy bears, jewellery, herbs and indigenous plants. You can grab something to eat at The Secret Garden Restaurant or at the Good Thyme Deli, both situated within the centre.

Tel number	011 967 1816
Address	40 High Road, Brentwood Park
GPS marker	26°07'25"S; 28°17'38"E
Opening hours	9am–5pm daily
Most appropriate age group	7+
Pram/wheelchair-friendly	Yes
Baby-changing facility	Yes
Nearest hospital	Netcare Linmed Hospital, 011 748 6200

Nearby

Visit/see: The Crucible, 8th Road, Rynpark, 011 969 6105.
Play/do: Little Feet Party Venue, 86B Miles Sharp Road, Rynfield, 079 398 7916.
Eat: The Parks Farm, 168 Kenmuir Street, Norton's Home Estates, 072 356 7816.
Shop: Lakeside Mall, Tom Jones Road, 011 427 1801.

Take note:
They hold a country market on the first and second Sunday of every month.

4 Wild Waters
www.wildwatersboksburg.co.za

5/5
Party venue rating

3/5
Rainy day option

Wild Waters is a family-friendly water park with a number of water activities, including a 500m super tube, raging rapids, a speed-hump slide, wave pool and calm pools for young children. They also have a putt putt course and a sandpit for volleyball. Take along your own food and make use of the picnic spots and braai facilities, or purchase a few snacks from the shop. The changing rooms are equipped with private lockers.

Tel number	011 826 6736
Address	Lozides Street, Boksburg
GPS marker	26°10'25"S; 28°14'37"E
Opening hours	10am–5pm daily; rides are turned off at 4pm
Most appropriate age group	3+
Pram/wheelchair-friendly	Yes
Baby-changing facility	Yes
Nearest hospital	Life The Glynnwood Hospital, 011 741 5000

Nearby
Visit/see: Petmasters Bird Park, 7 North Rand Road, Bartlett's, 011 894 2359, 011 918 3144. The South African Airways Museum Society, Dakota Crescent, Rand Airport, Germiston, 087 809 0224.
Play/do: Gumanji, Centric Park, corner North Rand and Romeo roads, Hughes, Boksburg, 073 202 2225.
Eat/play: Garden Shop Flora Farm, corner North Rand and Trichardt roads, Boksburg, 011 894 2377/8.

Take note:
The pools and attractions remain open during rain showers except during periods of lightning. Open from 1 September until the end of April.

COST
Adults and children 8 years and older R140, pensioners R85, children 2–7 years R75

Randburg/Rosebank/Sandton Area

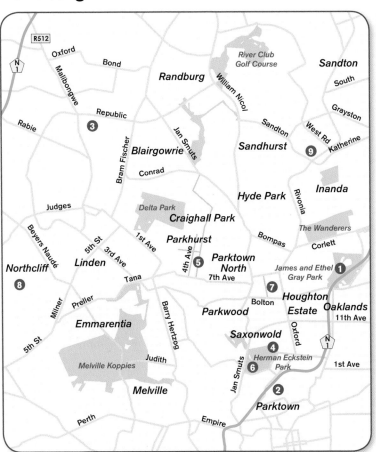

1. Acrobranch
2. Brenthurst Gardens
3. Brightwater Commons Shopping Centre
4. Ditsong National Museum of Military History
5. Fourth Avenue, Parkhurst
6. Joburg Zoo
7. Markets at Rosebank Mall
8. Northcliff Tower
9. Sandton City

1 Acrobranch
www.acrobranch.co.za

 5/5 Party venue rating

 3/5 Rainy day option

An aerial adventure park that takes children and adults from tree to tree using zip lines, Tarzan swings, nets, bridges and other fun obstacles. There are four courses, each designed with specific ages in mind, and a 200m zip line. Each course takes about two hours to complete and includes training and harnessing. There are additional parks in Pretoria, Cape Town and on the Garden Route. Each park offers catering and has a nearby restaurant. At the Joburg park they serve sweet and savoury crêpes.

COST R100–R250

Take note:
While there is a tuck shop for snacks, you might prefer to take a picnic to enjoy under the trees.

Tel number	086 999 0369, 010 593 0493
Address	James and Ethel Gray Park, Atholl-Oaklands Road, Melrose
GPS marker	26°08'29"S; 28°03'41"E
Opening hours	9am–5pm daily
Most appropriate age group	3+
Pram/wheelchair-friendly	Yes
Baby-changing facility	No
Nearest hospital	Netcare Rosebank Hospital, 011 328 0500

Nearby

Visit/see: Melrose Bird Sanctuary, James and Ethel Gray Park, 011 712 6600 (JHB City Parks). Wanderers Cricket Stadium, Corlett Drive, Illovo, 011 340 1500. Satyagraha House (Mohandas Gandhi Home), 15 Pine Road, Orchards, 011 485 5928.

Play/do: Kids Traffic Land, corner Louis Botha and Johannesburg roads, Balfour Park, 073 329 8510.

Shop: Melrose Arch Shopping Precinct, corner Corlett Drive and M1 Highway, Melrose, 011 684 0000. Blubird Shopping Centre, corner Atholl-Oaklands Road and Fort Street, Birnam, 011 887 2759.

Eat: Belle's Patisserie, Blubird Shopping Centre, corner Atholl-Oaklands Road and Fort Street, Birnam, 011 440 4474.

Sleep: Protea Hotel, Fire and Ice, 22 Whiteley Road, 011 218 4000.

2 Brenthurst Gardens
www.brenthurstgardens.co.za

0/5 Party venue rating

0/5 Rainy day option

The breathtaking Brenthurst Gardens are an 18ha private paradise attached to the Brenthurst Estate, the residence of the Oppenheimer family, founders of Anglo American in 1917. The gardens are mostly indigenous, with beautifully manicured lawns, stone pathways, fountains and the occasional sculpture to add to their appeal. The 45 gardeners tend the garden using organic methods and borehole water. Find out more during a guided walk led by the head gardener and horticulturalist. You need to book your visit a week in advance.

Tel number	011 646 4122
Address	1 Federation Road, Parktown
GPS marker	26°10'18"S; 28°02'38"E
Opening hours	October to April 10am–12pm Tuesday to Thursday; May to September 10am–12pm Wednesday and Thursday; closed in August
Most appropriate age group	6+
Pram/wheelchair-friendly	Yes
Baby-changing facility	No
Nearest hospital	Netcare Rosebank Hospital, 011 328 0500

Take note:
The money received from the entrance fee is donated to Little Eden, an organisation that cares for children and adults with intellectual disabilities.

Nearby

Visit/see: Munro Drive, Houghton.
Shop: Killarney Mall, Killarney Avenue, 011 646 4657.
For parents: The Munro Boutique Hotel, 63 St Patrick Road, Houghton Estate, 011 487 1420.

COST **R100 per person**

---

3 Brightwater Commons Shopping Centre

3/5 Party venue rating

4/5 Rainy day option

www.brightwatercommons.co.za

The Brightwater Commons Shopping Centre is made up of a ring of shops with the Randburg Flea Market, a grassy commons and musical fountains in the centre. Countless hours of entertainment can be had at the Boogaloos Skate Park, Adventure Golf, Laser Battle Zone, tenpin bowling alley and arcade. The centre hosts numerous events throughout the year.

Tel number	011 789 5052
Address	Republic Road, Randburg
GPS marker	26°06'14"S; 27°59'36"E
Closest public transport	Sandton Gautrain Station (17 minutes); take the S4 Gautrain Bus to Sandton; bus stop in the parking lot at the main entrance
Opening hours	9am–6pm Monday to Friday, 8am–6pm Saturday, 9am–3pm Sunday and public holidays; musical fountains: 7:30pm–7:45pm and 8:30pm–8:45pm Monday to Thursday, 7pm–7:45pm, 8pm–8:45pm and 9pm–9:45pm Friday to Sunday
Most appropriate age group	1+
Pram/wheelchair-friendly	Yes
Baby-changing facility	Yes
Nearest hospital	Mediclinic Sandton, 011 709 2000 Medicross Randburg, 011 796 1400

Nearby

Play/do: Environmental Centre and Delta Park, Road no. 3, Blairgowrie, 011 712 6600 (JHB City Parks).
Shop: Cresta Shopping Centre, corner Beyers Naudé Drive and Weltevreden Road, Cresta, 011 678 5306.

Take note: The centre regularly holds events in the centre court. Visit their website to find out what's happening during your visit.

4 Ditsong National Museum of Military History

3/5 Party venue rating

4/5 Rainy day option

www.ditsong.org.za

The National Museum of Military History, adjacent to the Joburg Zoo, was opened in 1947 by Jan Smuts. It was developed to serve as a memorial for all South Africans who have died in or as a result of military actions and to preserve our nation's military history for future generations. On a visit to the museum you can see the planes, tanks, submarines, arms and ammunition of the past. The striking Rand Regiments Memorial, with an angel on top of a dome, stands just outside the museum. It is dedicated to the men, women and children of all races and nations who lost their lives in the South African War.

Take note:
If you would like to hold a birthday party at the museum, they supply you with two tables and a maximum of 20 chairs. You can take photos outside the museum, but not in the hall.

Tel number	010 001 3515
Address	Erlswold Way, Saxonwold
GPS marker	26°09'47"S; 28°02'30"E
Opening hours	9am–4:30pm daily, excluding Good Friday, Christmas Day, and the first Sunday in September for Jazz on the Lake
Most appropriate age group	7+
Pram/wheelchair-friendly	Yes
Baby-changing facility	No
Nearest hospital	Netcare Rosebank Hospital, 011 328 0500

Nearby
Visit/see: Joburg Zoo, corner Jan Smuts Avenue and Upper Park Drive, Parktown, 011 646 2000.

COST Adults R30, pensioners R15, students and learners R25

---

5 Fourth Avenue, Parkhurst

0/5 Party venue rating

3/5 Rainy day option

www.4thavenue.co.za

Fourth Avenue in Parkhurst is a street lined with stylish shops, galleries, bakeries, several restaurants and cafés. Find a table on the sidewalk at one of the restaurants and watch the colourful characters go about their social rendezvous and errands.

Tel number	084 514 2884
Address	Fourth Avenue, Parkhurst
GPS marker	26°08'18"S; 28°01'04"E
Opening hours	Vary
Most appropriate age group	1+
Pram/wheelchair-friendly	Yes
Baby-changing facility	No
Nearest hospital	Netcare Rosebank Hospital, 011 328 0500

Take note:
If you're planning on going over the weekend, be sure to make a booking ahead of time at your restaurant of choice.

Nearby

Visit/see: Gallery Momo, 52 7th Avenue, 011 327 3247.
Eat: Vovo Telo, 4th Avenue, 011 447 5939. Angelo's Kitchen, 32 7th Avenue, 011 447 8001.
Shop: Senses Gift Gallery, 4th Avenue, 011 447 1961.
In Good Company, 52 6th Street, 011 447 1628.

COST
Varies

---

6 Joburg Zoo

www.jhbzoo.org.za

 3/5 Party venue rating

 2/5 Rainy day option

The Joburg Zoo houses over 320 animal species and can be explored by foot or on a ferry tour, which is a truck and trailer decorated in animal print. There are numerous themed enclosures housing animals indigenous to particular regions, such as Amazonia with animal species found in the Amazon, and Madagascar featuring unusual primates from that region. There are large lawns for picnicking, kiosks selling snacks, a restaurant and jungle gyms. Tours, talks and special events take place throughout the year.

COST
Adults R75; pensioners and students (weekdays only) and children 3–12 years R46

Tel number	011 646 2000
Address	Corner Jan Smuts Avenue and Upper Park Drive, Parktown
GPS marker	26°10'02"S; 28°02'14"E
Opening hours	8:30am–5:30pm daily, last entry 4pm
Most appropriate age group	3+
Pram/wheelchair-friendly	Yes
Baby-changing facility	No
Nearest hospital	Netcare Rosebank Hospital, 011 328 0500

Take note:
There are kiosks from which to purchase snacks, but take along your own food as they are quite expensive.

Nearby

Visit/see: The Ditsong National Museum of Military History, Erlswold Way, Saxonwold, 010 001 3515.
National Children's Theatre, 3 Junction Avenue, Parktown, 011 484 1584/5.
Play/do: Zoo Lake, Prince of Wales Drive, Parkview, 011 712 6600 (JHB City Parks).
Eat: Moyo, 1 Prince of Wales Drive, Parkview, 011 646 0058.
Sleep: Four Seasons Hotel Westcliff, 67 Jan Smuts Avenue, Westcliff, 011 481 6000.

7 Markets at Rosebank Mall
www.rosebankmall.co.za

 0/5 Party venue rating
 5/5 Rainy day option

The Rosebank Mall caters to a diverse clientele with its mix of fashion and accessory outlets, up-market restaurants, cafés and markets. The Arts and Crafts Market, situated on the ground level next to Europa, is open daily and offers an assortment of African art, tribal artefacts and indigenous curios. The Rosebank Sunday Market, situated on the rooftop, is only open on Sundays and here one will find bric-a-brac, antiques and collectibles, handmade products, clothing, jewellery as well as live music and food stalls.

COST Parking costs apply

Tel number	011 788 5530
Address	Bath Avenue, Rosebank
GPS marker	26°08'48"S; 28°02'28"E
Closest public transport	Rosebank Gautrain Station (one-minute walk)
Opening hours	Arts and Crafts Market: 9am–7pm Monday to Thursday, 9am–8pm Friday, 9am–6pm Saturday, 9am–5pm Sunday and public holidays; Rosebank Sunday Market: 9am–4pm every Sunday
Most appropriate age group	8+
Pram/wheelchair-friendly	Yes
Baby-changing facility	Yes
Nearest hospital	Netcare Rosebank Hospital, 011 328 0500

Nearby
Play/do: Color Café, Hyde Square Shopping Centre, Jan Smuts Avenue, Hyde Park, 011 341 0734.
Play/eat: Serendipity, 48 Keyes Avenue, 011 447 7386.
Eat: Piza-e-Vino, The Zone @ Rosebank, Oxford Road, 011 447 6569.
Wakaberry Frozen Yoghurt Bar, The Zone @ Rosebank, Oxford Road, 011 447 2790.

Take note: Be careful not to be ripped off simply because you're in a rush. Some vendors are open to negotiation.

---

8 Northcliff Tower
www.northcliffecopark.org

 1/5 Party venue rating
 0/5 Rainy day option

Experience breathtaking 360° views of Joburg from the second-highest point of the city, Northcliff Ridge. The Northcliff Ridge Eco Park area is controlled by City Parks and Joburg Water, which have a large water tower, built in 1939, on the very top of the ridge. The area is fenced off and locked in the evening and there is a guard at the parking area.

Take note: Although there is a security guard, it is recommended that you travel in a group and don't take valuables with you.

Tel number	011 021 0000, 083 407 6590
Address	Park in Lucky Avenue, Northcliff
GPS marker	26°08'45"S; 27°58'12"E
Opening hours	Sunrise to sunset
Most appropriate age group	6+
Pram/wheelchair-friendly	No
Baby-changing facility	No
Nearest hospital	Life Flora Clinic, 011 470 7777

Nearby

Play/do: Orango Tango's, Northcliff Corner Shopping Centre, corner Beyers Naudé Drive and Milner Avenue, 011 782 3917, 084 775 9797.
Eat: Lambrusco's Italian Dining, 5/6 Fir Drive Centre, corner Fir Drive and Weltevreden Road, 011 431 0591. Isabella's Food and Cake Shop, Northcliff Square Centre, corner Milner Avenue and Beyers Naudé Drive, Northcliff, 011 888 8234. Petits Fours Paris, corner Beyers Naudé and Castle Hill drives, Northcliff, 011 431 0319.
Shop: World Wear Shopping Centre, corner Beyers Naudé Drive and Wilson Road, Fairland, 011 684 1916.

---

9 Sandton City
www.sandtoncity.com

This is a prestigious shopping centre with close to 300 local and international retailers, restaurants and coffee shops. Adjacent to the centre is Nelson Mandela Square, which is home to the Theatre on the Square, a 6m bronzed statue of Nelson Mandela, additional retailers and restaurants and the Sandton Library.

Take note: Watch your children as the mall can get quite busy on weekends. Themed activities are held in the Checkers Court during the school holidays.

COST — Parking costs apply

Tel number	011 217 6000
Address	83 Rivonia Road, corner Sandton Drive, Sandton
GPS marker	26°06'32"S; 28°03'05"E
Closest public transport	At Gautrain Station Sandton (a three-minute walk)
Opening hours	9am–8pm Monday to Saturday, 9am–6pm Sunday and public holidays
Most appropriate age group	7+
Pram/wheelchair-friendly	Yes
Baby-changing facility	Yes
Nearest hospital	Mediclinic Morningside, 011 282 5000

Nearby

Visit/see: Art Afrique Gallery, Level 4 Legacy Corner, corner Maude and 5th streets, 011 292 7113. Sandton Convention Centre, 161 Maude Street, 011 779 0000.
Play/do: Build-A-Bear Workshop, Shop C3, Sandton City, 011 883 0911.
Eat: Papachinos Italian Restaurant, corner Rivonia Road and Cullinan Close, Morningside, 011 783 1090.
For parents: San Deck Bar and Restaurant, Sandton Sun, corner Fifth and Alice streets, 011 780 5000.

Northern Johannesburg

1. Bounce Inc
2. Bryanston Organic and Natural Market
3. Chartwell Castle
4. Jozi X
5. Liliesleaf Farm
6. Lipizzaner Centre
7. Montecasino
8. PwC Bike Park
9. StokeCity WakePark
10. The Dome
11. The Lonehill Nature Reserve

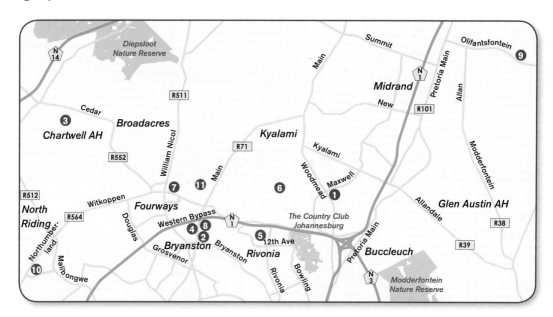

---

1 Bounce Inc
www.bounceinc.co.za

5/5 Party venue rating
5/5 Rainy day option

A high-energy trampoline centre with more than 100 interconnected trampolines surrounded by gymnastics-grade padding, giant airbags and springs. Young and old can try their hand at free jumping, aerial tricks, slam dunking, wall running and dodgeball. There is a dedicated free jumping area for children three years and older and under 110cm in height. Safety is a priority and classes in learning to jump safely as well as specialised aerial training classes are available for all levels.

Tel number	011 517 2500
Address	Waterfall Lifestyle Estate, corner Woodmead and Maxwell drives, Jukskei Ext. 50, Midrand
GPS marker	26°01'13"S; 28°05'17"E
Opening hours	10am–10pm Monday to Friday (school and public holidays 9am–10pm), 8am–10pm Saturdays, 8am–8pm Sundays
Most appropriate age group	3+
Pram/wheelchair-friendly	Yes
Baby-changing facility	No
Nearest hospital	Netcare Waterfall City Hospital, 011 304 6600

Nearby

Eat: Vovo Telo bakery and café, Waterfall Corner, Waterfall Lifestyle Estate, Midrand, 010 596 1355. Wakaberry Frozen Yoghurt Bar, Waterfall Corner, Waterfall Lifestyle Estate, Midrand, 010 596 8953.

Shop: PartySpot, Woodmead Value Mart, Waterval Crescent, Woodmead, 011 804 5143.

Take note:
All jumpers are required to wear grip socks designed to help maximise grip, safety and general hygiene.

COST — General access R140; junior jumpers R100; students R90 (Monday to Friday); group sessions from R115; parties from R200/person

---

2. Bryanston Organic and Natural Market

www.bryanstonorganicmarket.co.za

0/5 Party venue rating

2/5 Rainy day option

A well-known market that sells organic produce and natural, hand-made crafts. The market is set on the grounds of the Michael Mount Waldorf School and takes place twice a week. It started in 1976 when a group of parents organised a fair to raise money for the school. At the end of the fair there were lots of vegetables left over, which were sold to other parents in the school. This became a regular occurrence, with organic farmers selling produce from their car boots, and has since evolved into the thriving market that it is today.

Take note:
Festive Moonlight Markets take place from mid-November until Christmas.

Tel number	011 706 3671
Address	40 Culross Road, Bryanston
GPS marker	26°02'41"S; 28°01'40"E
Opening hours	9am–3pm Thursday, Saturday and public holidays
Most appropriate age group	1+
Pram/wheelchair-friendly	Yes
Baby-changing facility	Yes
Nearest hospital	Mediclinic Sandton, 011 709 2000

Nearby

Play/do: PWC Cycle Park, 1A Libertas Street, off Sloane Street, 083 725 BIKE (2453). Slackline Park, Jozi X Adventure Centre, corner Main Road and Sloane Street, 082 456 2358.

Eat: Petits Fours Milan, Bryanston Shopping Centre, corner Ballyclare and William Nicol drives, 011 514 0932. Junipa's Bistro and Café, Hobart Grove Centre, corner Hobart and Grosvenor roads, 011 706 2387, 011 706 0479.

3 Chartwell Castle
www.chartwellcastle.co.za

 4/5 Party venue rating

 0/5 Rainy day option

Located on the Klein Jukskei River, this four-storey castle provides accommodation and caters for various functions, including weddings. On the 5ha plot you will find the biggest known uninterrupted hedgerow maze in the southern hemisphere, boasting more than 900 conifers. The public is welcome to take along picnics and enjoy a day in the maze.

Tel number	010 227 0002, 079 310 1156
Address	1 Hood Road, corner Watercombe Road, Chartwell West
GPS marker	25°58'58"S; 27°57'41"E
Opening hours	8am–4pm daily
Most appropriate age group	3–10
Pram/wheelchair-friendly	Yes
Baby-changing facility	Yes
Nearest hospital	Life Fourways Hospital, 011 875 1000

COST Adults R50, children under 12 R25

Nearby
Play/do: Seedpod Studio, Broadacres Lifestyle Centre, Cedar Road, 011 465 0375.
Eat/play: D'Ouwe Werf, Broadacres Lifestyle Centre, Cedar Road, 011 540 1538. Mugg & Bean, Broadacres Lifestyle Centre, Cedar Road, 011 465 0155.

4 Jozi X
www.jozix.co.za

 5/5 Party venue rating

 0/5 Rainy day option

This park caters to anyone with a sense of adventure. They have an Adventure World with eight different harness-free activities, including a 9m climbing wall, a circus-sized trapeze and a slip 'n slide. The Slackline Park gets you to perfect your balance while making your way across flexible pieces of webbing, set at different heights. They also offer mountain boarding, a big air cushion that allows people to safely learn tricks on their bikes, boards and blades, a parkour gymnasium and bubble soccer.

COST Big Air Krush Kushion Jump: R50 for three hours; bubble soccer: one hour exclusively R1,500 (4 x 10-minute games), two hours exclusively R2,200 (8 x 10-minute games), or 15 minutes R50 per person, 30 minutes R80 per person

COST Action World: R100 Wednesday to Friday, R120 Saturday and Sunday; Slackline Park: R50 per session Saturday and Sunday; Mountain boarding: R250 for a two-hour lesson, includes equipment and slope pass; equipment rental R150 per day, slope pass R100 per day

Tel number	082 456 2358
Address	Corner Main Road and Sloane Street, Bryanston
GPS marker	26°02'18"S; 28°01'30"E
Opening hours	Action World: 10am–5pm Wednesday to Sunday; Slackline Park: 10am–1pm and 1pm–4pm (two sessions) Saturday and Sunday; Big Air Krush Kushion Jump: 1pm–5pm Saturday
Most appropriate age group	5+
Pram/wheelchair-friendly	No
Baby-changing facility	No
Nearest hospital	Life Fourways Hospital, 011 875 1000

Take note: Take along your swimming costumes and towels for the slip 'n slide that runs from September/October until mid-May. Take your own food and drinks. They don't have an ATM.

---

5 Liliesleaf Farm
www.liliesleaf.co.za

0/5
Party venue rating

5/5
Rainy day option

Liliesleaf Farm is a site that played a prominent role during the liberation struggle in the 1960s. The farm was used as a meeting place for the underground Communist Party and Umkhonto we Sizwe (MK) high command, and was a safe house for political fugitives. In 1963 the police raided the farm, arrested senior ANC members and found hundreds of incriminating documents, subsequently leading to the Rivonia Trial and the arrest of Nelson Mandela. The farm is now a Heritage Site and an interactive museum. Visitors are welcome to explore the museum at their own pace and get insights into some of the revolutionary personalities who helped shape South Africa's democracy, or else join a guided tour.

COST
Self-guided tours: adults R80, children 8 years and older and pensioners R40, children 0–7 years free; guided tours: adults R130, students R60, children 8 years and older and pensioners R40, children 0–7 years free

Tel number	011 803 7882/3/4
Address	7 George Avenue, Rivonia
GPS marker	26°02'38"S; 28°03'13"E
Opening hours	8:30am–5pm Monday to Friday, 9am–4pm Saturday, Sunday and public holidays; closed 24, 25, 26 December and 1 January
Most appropriate age group	12+
Pram/wheelchair-friendly	Yes
Baby-changing facility	No
Nearest hospital	Netcare Sunninghill Hospital, 011 806 1672

Nearby
Play/do: Yeesh! Fun for Kids, Unit G6, Woodmead Commercial Park, Waterfall Crescent, Woodmead, 011 656 9669.
Eat: Da Vincenzo Italian Restaurant, 29 Montrose Road, Sunninghill, 011 466 2618/42. Adega Rivonia, Rivonia Crossing 2, 3 Achter Road, corner Witkoppen and Rivonia roads, Sandton, 087 550 4377.
For parents: Sir James van der Merwe, 6 Desmond Street, Kramerville, 072 607 4235.

Take note:
There is an on-site restaurant that serves light meals and refreshments.

---

6 Lipizzaner Centre
www.lipizzaners.co.za

 3/5 Party venue rating   **5/5** Rainy day option

Enjoy a performance by the magnificent white Lipizzaner stallions, and visit the stable courtyard after the show to meet the riders and feed carrots to the horses. The Lipizzaner equestrian centre in Kyalami was established in 1960 by Major George Iwanowski, a Polish cavalry officer who trained the first stallion, Maestoso Erdem, in high school dressage movements. Dressage is a highly disciplined equestrian sport that requires the horse to perform a series of movements that give the impression that the horse is dancing.

COST: Adults and children 13 years and older R140, pensioners R80, children 4–12 years R80, children 0–3 years free; special performance costs vary

Tel number	079 716 4792
Address	1 Dahlia Road, Kyalami
GPS marker	25°58'13"S; 28°03'17"E
Opening hours	10:30am every Sunday
Most appropriate age group	3+
Pram/wheelchair-friendly	Yes
Baby-changing facility	No
Nearest hospital	Netcare Waterfall City Hospital, 011 304 6600
	Life Carstenhof Clinic, 011 655 5500

Nearby
Visit/see: Mapatiza, Underground Gemstone Tours, 52 Mercury Avenue, Crowthorne, 011 468 1467.
Eat: Papachinos Italian Restaurant, 40 Whisken Avenue, Crowthorne, 011 702 1234.

Take note:
Those wishing to have their birthday party at the centre can set up in the court-yard after the performance. They have a party planner who can assist with all the arrangements, and they supply a jumping castle.

7 Montecasino
www.montecasino.co.za

 3/5 Party venue rating

 5/5 Rainy day option

This is an enclosed entertainment centre designed to replicate a Tuscan village, with cobblestone streets, washing lines strung between passageways, pigeons roosting in the eaves and even a painted sky that imitates the setting sun. In keeping with the theme, entertainers occasionally stroll the streets, and there are buskers at points throughout the centre. There are several restaurants, a cinema complex, tenpin bowling alley, laser tag, an arcade, two theatres and the Montecasino Bird Gardens. The Bird Gardens feature a variety of colourful birds, mammals, reptiles and unusual animals from around the world, and the Flight of Fantasy bird show is held here daily.

Tel number	011 510 7000
Address	Corner William Nicol Drive and Witkoppen Road, Fourways, Sandton
GPS marker	26°01'32"S; 28°00'45"E
Closest public transport	Sandton Gautrain Station (22 minutes); take the S5 Gautrain Bus; bus stop in the Montecasino Palazzo Circle
Opening hours	Restaurants and shops: 10am–10pm Monday to Friday, 10am–12pm Saturday and Sunday; the casino is open 24/7; Montecasino Bird Gardens: 8:30am–5pm Monday to Friday, 8:30am–6pm Saturday, Sunday and public holidays; Flight of Fantasy bird show: 11am and 3pm Monday to Friday, 11am, 1pm and 3pm Saturday, Sunday and public holidays
Most appropriate age group	1+
Pram/wheelchair-friendly	Yes
Baby-changing facility	Yes
Nearest hospital	Mediclinic Sandton, 011 709 2000

Nearby

Play/do: Avalanche, Cedar Square, Cedar Road, Fourways, 011 467 2426. Play at Height, Pineslopes Shopping Centre Casino View, corner Witkoppen Road and The Straight, Fourways, 072 534 7911.

Play/eat: Smile Café, Cedar Square Shopping Centre, corner Cedar Road and Fourways Boulevard, Fourways, 011 465 4162. Papachinos Italian restaurant, Sevens Decor Centre, corner The Straight and Witkoppen Road, Pineslopes, 011 467 4460. Fourways Farmer's Market, corner Montecasino Boulevard and William Nicol Drive, Fourways, 011 465 5276. Montecasino (Spur, Ciao Baby, Col'Cacchio, Mugg & Bean and Gourmet Garage), 011 510 7000.

Shop/eat: FreeRange Lifestyle Centre's The Lot Restaurant and Pangolin Toy Store, Rustic Timber and Garden Centre, 42 Witkoppen Road, Fourways, 011 465 5193.

Sleep: The Palazzo Montecasino, Southern Sun Montecasino, and Sun Square Montecasino, 011 510 7000.

For parents: Casa Del Sol Restaurant, Olivedale Corner Shopping Centre, Olivedale, 011 704 6493.

COST — Parking R10 per car, flat rate

Take note: You will be searched for weapons and illegal gambling devices upon entry.

8 PwC Bike Park
www.bikepark.co.za

  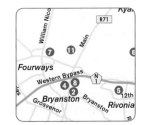

This is an international-standard cycle park with a variety of activities suitable for the whole family. There is a tarred track for young children starting out on a pushbike or training wheels, a junior mountain-bike trail, pump track and a multi-tiered BMX track. Spectators can watch the cyclists from the clubhouse deck or from picnic spots on the grass embankment.

Tel number	083 725 BIKE (2453)
Address	1A Libertas Street, off Sloane Street, Bryanston
GPS marker	26°02'10"S; 28°01'41"E
Opening hours	6am–6pm daily
Most appropriate age group	4+
Pram/wheelchair-friendly	Yes
Baby-changing facility	No
Nearest hospital	Mediclinic Sandton, 011 709 2000

COST: Adults R60, children under 12 years R50, children under 5 years R20; bike hire: mountain bikes R200 per day, BMX R100 per day

Nearby
Eat: Junipa's Bistro and Café, Hobart Grove Centre, corner Hobart and Grosvenor roads, 011 706 2387, 011 706 0479.
Shop: Bryanston Organic and Natural Market, 40 Culross Road, Bryanston, 011 706 3671.
Play/do: RollEgoli roller rink, 296 Main Road, Bryanston, 083 232 9861.

Take note:
If you don't own your own bike, don't stress. They have a selection of mountain bikes, BMX bikes or children's straddle bikes available for hire. No helmet, no ride.

---

9 StokeCity WakePark
www.stokecity.co.za

Learn to water-ski, wakeboard, wakeskate and kneeboard at this cable park. They also have a swimming pool, jungle gym, volleyball court, skate park, and braai and picnic facilities. The park has a two-tower cable system, which is suitable for beginners. After you have fallen, a cable will be used to collect you while you wait in the water in your life jacket. They also have a five-tower cable system for more advanced riders who need to swim to the side of the dam after they have fallen.

Tel number	011 314 3589
Address	Corner R562 and Olifantsfontein Road, Glen Austin
GPS marker	25°56'50"S; 28°11'17"E
Opening hours	12pm–6pm Tuesday to Friday, 10am–6pm Saturday and Sunday; closed on Mondays; closed June to August
Most appropriate age group	6+
Pram/wheelchair-friendly	Yes
Baby-changing facility	Yes
Nearest hospital	Life Carstenhof Clinic, 011 655 5500

COST

General admission R30 per person, children under 6 years free, cable pass from R180, cable pass and board hire from R250

Nearby

Visit/see: Lory Park, Animal and Owl Sanctuary, 180/1 Kruger Road, President Park, Midrand, 011 315 7307.

Eat: Harvard Café, Grand Central Airport, New Road, 011 805 8657.

Take note:
You need to be able to swim to take part in any of the water activities. Take along charcoal and firelighters if you want to make use of their braai facilities. You are not allowed to bring drinks into the park.

---

(10) The Dome

www.ticketprodome.co.za

0/5 Party venue rating

5/5 Rainy day option

The Dome is a premier event venue that hosts many expos, trade shows and music concerts. The venue is visible from across the countryside due to its white-domed roof. Their private baby-feeding area, sponsored by Philips Avent, is event specific.

Tel number	011 794 5800
Address	Corner Northumberland and Olievenhout avenues, North Riding
GPS marker	26°03'48"S; 27°56'36"E
Opening hours	Show times vary
Most appropriate age group	11+
Pram/wheelchair-friendly	Yes
Baby-changing facility	Yes
Nearest hospital	Life Flora Clinic, 011 470 7777 (during shows, the Dome has a fully equipped medical clinic situated on the right-hand side of the stage)

COST

Show costs vary

Nearby

Play/do: Northgate Ice Rink, Northgate Shopping Centre, Northumberland Road, North Riding, 011 794 8706.

Eat/play: Lone Wolf Spur, corner Eastwood Avenue and Knoppiesdoring Street, Randpark Ridge, 011 794 9791.

Lifestyle Garden Centre, Beyers Naudé Drive, 011 792 5616.

Take note:
You are not permitted to take your own food or drinks into the venue. There are two ATMs within the venue and several food and drink vendors.

---

11 The Lonehill Nature Reserve

www.jhbcityparks.com

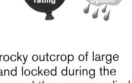

The Lonehill Nature Reserve is known for the rocky outcrop of large boulders called tor rocks. The area is fenced and locked during the week, but on weekends you are able to walk around the reserve, climb to the top to enjoy the views, and picnic on the lawns. The reserve is home to numerous dassies, guinea fowl and porcupines. There is a fenced play park near the reserve, and a dam that contains bass, barbel and carp.

Tel number	011 712 6600
Address	Calderwood Road, Lonehill
GPS marker	26°01'07"S; 28°01'39"E
Opening hours	7am–6pm Saturday, Sunday and public holidays
Most appropriate age group	6+
Pram/wheelchair-friendly	No
Baby-changing facility	No
Nearest hospital	Life Fourways Hospital, 011 875 1000

Nearby

Play/do: Montecasino Entertainment Centre, corner William Nicol Drive and Witkoppen Road, 011 510 7000.

Shop: Lonehill Shopping Centre, Lonehill Boulevard, 083 414 7202.

For parents: The Steamworks Gastropub, corner Sunset Avenue and Forest Drive, 011 467 9721.

Take note:
There are toilets and baby-changing facilities at the Lonehill Shopping Centre.

West Rand

① Croc City
② Honeydew A-Maize-Ing Mazes
③ Krugersdorp Museum
④ Lion Park
⑤ Magaliesberg Canopy Tour

⑥ Mountain Sanctuary Park
⑦ The Maropeng Visitor Centre
⑧ The Other Side Restaurant
⑨ Walter Sisulu National Botanical Garden
(WSNBG)

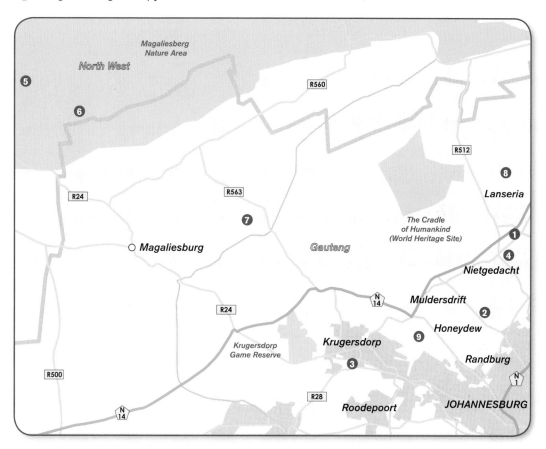

① Croc City
croccity.co.za

4/5 Party venue rating
1/5 Rainy day option

Take an informative guided tour of the Croc City Crocodile and Reptile Park, where you will have the opportunity to hold a baby crocodile, various exotic snakes and even a tarantula. Brave adults and children who weigh 20kg or more can enjoy an aerial view of the three Nile crocodile enclosures while on the FlyOver, a zip line that suspends visitors 5m above the hungry predators. If children under 20kg want to give it a go, they can go in tandem with one of the trained guides. Snake shows and crocodile feeding take place on weekends.

Take note:
Try their speciality pizzas with croc meat.

Tel number	083 321 1016, 083 657 7561
Address	Plot 59, corner Cedar Road and R114, Nietgedacht
GPS marker	25°58'37"S; 27°56'40"E
Opening hours	9am–4:30pm daily; croc feeding: 2pm Saturday and Sunday; venomous snake show: 11am–12pm Sundays and public holidays
Most appropriate age group	4+
Pram/wheelchair-friendly	Yes
Baby-changing facility	Yes
Nearest hospital	Life Fourways Hospital, 011 875 1000

Nearby
Play/do: Northern Farm Nature Reserve, off the R144 to Diepsloot, 083 879 4449.

COST: Entrance fee: adults R70, pensioners R60, children under 12 years R50; FlyOver: adults R95, children 12 years and older R75

2 Honeydew A-Maize-Ing Mazes

www.honeydewmazes.co.za

5/5 Party venue rating

0/5 Rainy day option

This is a giant maze and a fun quiz trail for children and adults alike. From about March to May each year, a maze formed by living maize plants is opened to the public. The maze follows a new theme each year and the 10 stations with mind-boggling quizzes that are dotted throughout the maze change regularly to stay challenging. During the rest of the year, while the maize is being harvested and replanted, an Elemental Maze made from reed walls provides just as much entertainment. There's a tuck shop selling sweets and snacks, and shaded benches and plenty of space to lay out a picnic blanket on the lawns.

COST: Adults and children over 15 years R120, children 15 years and under R100

Take note:
The living maze runs from March to May. No children under the age of 15 are allowed into this maze without adult supervision. Moonlight Mazes take place on select nights in the year, such as on Halloween.

Tel number	073 795 2174
Address	82 Boland Street, just off Beyers Naudé Drive, Honeydew
GPS marker	27°54'07"S; 26°03'16"E
Opening hours	10am–5pm Saturday and Sunday, last entries 2:30pm
Most appropriate age group	7+
Pram/wheelchair-friendly	Yes
Baby-changing facility	No
Nearest hospital	Life Flora Clinic, 011 470 7777

Nearby

Eat: Alfresco Italian Restaurant (across the road from Honeydew Mazes), Plot 41, Boland Street, 011 794 4388, 011 794 5475. Trés Jolie, Plot 22, Peter Road, Ruimsig, 011 026 0153, 079 527 5008. Casalinga Ristorante Italiano, Rocky Ridge Road, off Beyers Naudé Drive, Muldersdrift, 011 957 2612/3311.

 # Krugersdorp Museum

www.mogalecity.gov.za

0/5 Party venue rating

5/5 Rainy day option

The museum touches on the history and cultures of Mogale City, from the tools used by the Batswana in the Stone Age, the make-shift knives that date back to the Iron Age, the reeds used to secure households during the South African War, and the history of mining. There is a colourful children's section with toys from the past on display. The museum is housed within the old Magistrate's Court, a Republican-style building whose cornerstone was laid on 18 September 1890 by President Paul Kruger. The building is situated next to the old post and telegraph office.

Tel number	011 951 2000/2336
Address	Corner Commissioner and Monument streets, Krugersdorp
GPS marker	26°06'07"S; 27°46'19"E
Opening hours	9:30am–4pm Monday to Friday, 9am–12pm Saturday
Most appropriate age group	9+
Pram/wheelchair-friendly	Yes
Baby-changing facility	No
Nearest hospital	Netcare Krugersdorp Hospital, 011 951 0200 Life Robinson Private Hospital, 011 278 8700

Take note:
The Krugersdorp Town Hall is situated directly across from the museum.

Nearby

Visit/see: Krugersdorp Game Reserve, Rustenburg Road, 071 556 3813.
Play/do: Bungee Mogale, Wolf Street, 0861 128 6344, 011 660 7378.
Pines Resort (closed in winter), 2 Ivan Smuts Ave, Silverfields, 011 955 3845.
Eat/sleep: The Rabbit Hole Hotel and Restaurant, 33 Viljoen Street, 011 665 3242.
Shop: Key West Shopping Centre, Paardekraal Drive, 011 273 0400. Cradlestone Mall, Furrow Road, 010 020 1234.
For parents: Greensleeves Medieval Kingdom, Hekpoort Road, R563, Sterkfontein, 082 602 2958.

Lion Park
(4) *www.lion-park.com*

5/5
Party venue rating

3/5
Rainy day option

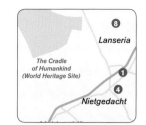

The park is home to more than 85 lions, including rare white lions, as well as cheetah, wild dog and various hyena species. You have the option of a self-drive tour, a day or night guided tour in their safari vehicle, or a photographic tour in their silent electric vehicle. Please take note of the park rules, such as keeping car windows closed at all times. The park offers lion cub, giraffe and ostrich interactions, a cheetah walk, a fun-filled children's playground with a variety of jungle gyms, jumping castles, entertaining rides, and a restaurant. Their optional door-to-door shuttle service will collect you from your hotel, airport, home or any other location and take you back safely after your visit.

Tel number	087 150 0100, 011 691 9905
Address	Lanseria
GPS marker	Phone for directions
Opening hours	8:30am–9pm daily; lion feeding: 12pm Saturday and Sunday
Most appropriate age group	4+
Pram/wheelchair-friendly	Yes
Baby-changing facility	Yes
Nearest hospital	Life Flora Clinic, 011 470 7777

Take note:
If you prefer to miss the crowds and navigate the park freely, avoid visiting on Sundays at noon as this is when they feed the lions. You can witness a feeding on a guided night drive at 6:30pm or 7:30pm Monday to Sunday and 11:30am Saturday and Sunday.

COST Self-drive: adults R160, with cub interaction R200, children 4–12 years R60–R80, with cub interaction R90–R110, children under 4 years free; giraffe and ostrich feed R30 per bag; shuttle service: rates vary depending on distance

Nearby
<u>Visit/see</u>: Ngwenya Glass Village, Shady Lane, off Diepsloot R114, Muldersdrift, 082 785 7397.
<u>Play/do</u>: Brookwood Estate Trout Farm, R374, Muldersdrift, 011 957 0126. Gnu Kids, Plot 78 Swartkop, Muldersdrift, 074 920 7786. Hero Adventure Park, Heia Safari, 1747 Beyers Naudé Drive, Muldersdrift, 011 919 5000. Avianto, Plot 69, R114, Muldersdrift, 011 668 3000.
<u>Eat/shop</u>: Garden World, Beyers Naudé Drive, Muldersdrift, 011 957 2046.
<u>Shop</u>: Kiddies' Superstore at the Lion Park, Lanseria, 087 150 0100, 011 691 9905.
<u>Sleep</u>: Wild Side tented camp at the Lion Park, Lanseria, 087 150 0100, 011 691 9905.

5 Magaliesberg Canopy Tour

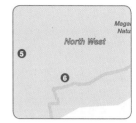

4/5 Party venue rating

1/5 Rainy day option

www.magaliescanopytour.co.za

An eco-adventure that takes you zip lining across 11 platforms that have been erected against the rock faces of the Ysterhout Kloof. The cables span 140m in length, and in places you dangle 140m above the canopy floor. You are accompanied by two trained guides to ensure your safety and enjoyment. The tours are suitable for children from about four or five years old, as long as they fit the harness, and for people who weigh no more than 120kg.

Take note: Wear comfortable clothing and closed shoes.

Tel number	014 535 0150, 079 492 0467
Address	Sparkling Waters Hotel and Spa, off the N4 to Rustenburg
GPS marker	25°49'51"S; 27°24'43"E
Opening hours	Summer 6:30am–4:30pm daily, winter 7am–3pm daily; tours depart at 30-minute intervals; closed Christmas Day
Most appropriate age group	5+
Pram/wheelchair-friendly	No
Baby-changing facility	No
Nearest hospital	Netcare Ferncrest Hospital, 014 568 4399

COST R495 per person

Nearby
Visit/see: Mountain Sanctuary Park, off the N4 to Rustenburg, 014 534 0114, 082 707 5538. Eat: Askari Lodge, 1 Doornspruit Road, Doornhoek, Magaliesburg, 014 577 2658/9. Black Horse Estate, 32 Zeekoeihoek Road, Magaliesburg, 082 453 5295. Goblin's Cove Fantasy Restaurant, Bekker Schools Road, Hekpoort, 014 576 2143, 081 043 1155.

Special event
Cellar Rats in May and September – annual wine festival with supervised children's activities

6 Mountain Sanctuary Park

3/5 Party venue rating

1/5 Rainy day option

www.mountain-sanctuary.co.za

This privately owned nature reserve welcomes weekend visitors, who can spend the night in one of several self-catering cabins and chalets, as well as a restricted number of day visitors. Nature lovers can spend their time hiking and swimming in the crystal-clear mountain rock pools, rock climbing, abseiling and mountain biking. The park has a swimming pool, braai facilities and a lapa available to hire for functions.

COST
Day visitors: adults R100, children 2–12 years R60, R35 per vehicle

Tel number	014 534 0114, 082 707 5538
Address	Off the N4 to Rustenburg
GPS marker	25°50'10"S; 27°28'33"E
Opening hours	8am–5pm daily
Most appropriate age group	6+
Pram/wheelchair-friendly	Yes
Baby-changing facility	No
Nearest hospital	Netcare Ferncrest Hospital, 014 568 4399

Take note:
Phone ahead as they only allow 180 visitors into the park each day, which includes those seeking accommodation and arriving with campers.

Nearby
Play/do: Magaliesberg Canopy Tour, departs from Sparkling Waters Hotel and Spa, off the N4 to Rustenburg, 014 535 0150, 079 492 0467.
For parents: Brauhaus am Damm, R24, 087 802 5519.

7 The Maropeng Visitor Centre
www.maropeng.co.za

5/5 Party venue rating
1/5 Rainy day option

The centre details the origins of humankind. On arrival, visitors will see a massive burial mound called the Tumulus, which houses the Maropeng exhibition and the Tumulus Restaurant. Self-guided tours start with a boat ride through the various stages of the Earth's creation and progress to interactive displays addressing the evolutionary journey of humankind, discussing the controlled use of fire, the development of stone tools and language, and more. Guided tours are offered over the weekend and on public holidays.

COST
Adults R160, pensioners R85, students R100, children 4–14 years R90, children under 4 years free; combination ticket (Maropeng and Sterkfontein Caves): adults R215, children 4–14 years R143, children under 4 years free

Take note:
Combine your visit to the Maropeng Visitor Centre with a trip to the Sterkfontein Caves. No pets are allowed.

Tel number	014 577 9000
Address	R563, Hekpoort Road, Sterkfontein
GPS marker	25°58'01"S; 27°39'45"E
Opening hours	9am–5pm daily; last boat ride at 4pm
Most appropriate age group	7+
Pram/wheelchair-friendly	Yes
Baby-changing facility	Yes
Nearest hospital	Netcare Krugersdorp Hospital, 011 951 0200

Nearby

<u>Visit/see</u>: Sterkfontein Caves, Kromdraai Road, Cradle of Humankind, 014 577 9000. Rhino and Lion Nature Reserve, 520 Kromdraai Road, Cradle of Humankind, 011 957 0106.
<u>Play/do</u>: Wild Cave Adventures, Cradle of Humankind, 011 956 6197.
<u>Eat</u>: Le Sel @ The Cradle Restaurant, Route T9, Kromdraai Road, 011 659 1622. The Market Place Restaurant and Tumulus Restaurant at the Maropeng Visitor Centre, 014 577 9000.
<u>Sleep</u>: Maropeng Boutique Hotel, 014 577 9000.
<u>For parents</u>: Roots Restaurant, Letamo Game Estate, Kromdraai Road, 011 668 7000.

Special event
The Winter Sculpture Fair (May) at Nirox Foundation Sculpture Park

---

8 The Other Side Restaurant
www.monaghanfarm.co.za

5/5 Party venue rating 3/5 Rainy day option

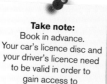

This informal restaurant on a working farm serves a sumptuous buffet lunch on Sundays. Children can take along their bicycles and enjoy the freedom of wide-open spaces as they explore the farm. There is also a jungle gym and, in the summer months, a water slide.

Take note:
Book in advance. Your car's licence disc and your driver's licence need to be valid in order to gain access to the farm.

COST Food costs vary; Sunday buffet: adults from R255, children from R130

Tel number	087 260 4130, 078 411 4886
Address	Monaghan Farms, off Ashanti Road, Lanseria
GPS marker	25°54'57"S; 27°55'38"E
Opening hours	8am–5pm Tuesday and Thursday, 8am–8pm Wednesday and Friday (bar closes at 9pm), 8am–4pm Saturday, 8am–10:30am and 1pm–3pm Sunday
Most appropriate age group	4+
Pram/wheelchair-friendly	Yes
Baby-changing facility	Yes
Nearest hospital	Life Fourways Hospital, 011 875 1000

Nearby
<u>Play/eat</u>: Stornoway Lodge with Old MacDonald's Party Farm and The Fat Olive Restaurant, Portion 123 and 125, Farm Lindley, Pelindaba Road (R512), Lanseria, 071 354 6622.
<u>Eat</u>: Maggie's Farm Restaurant, Home of the Chicken Pie, Pelindaba Road (R512), Lanseria, 082 651 8844.

⑨ Walter Sisulu National Botanical Garden (WSNBG)
www.sanbi.org

3/5 Party venue rating

1/5 Rainy day option

Nestled among the Roodepoort Hills, the WSNBG boasts indigenous gardens, a waterfall, rock pools, a bird hide, a children's playground and a green gym with a variety of outdoor equipment. The Eagle Express train runs on weekends and ferries people from the entrance of the gardens to the waterfall. The gardens are home to a breeding pair of Verreaux's eagles that nest on the cliffs alongside the waterfall. There are a number of reptiles and small mammals to see too. The gardens hold numerous talks, walks and music concerts throughout the year.

Tel number	086 100 1278
Address	End of Malcolm Road, Poortview, Roodepoort
GPS marker	27°50'41"S; 26°05'14"E
Opening hours	8am–5pm daily; Eagle Express operates from 12pm, Saturday, Sunday and public holidays
Most appropriate age group	3–10
Pram/wheelchair-friendly	Yes
Baby-changing facility	Yes
Nearest hospital	Life Flora Clinic, 011 470 7777

Nearby

Visit/see: Confidence Reef at Kloofendal Nature Reserve, corner Galena Avenue and Veronica Street, Kloofendal, 011 674 2980, 079 693 5608.

Play: The Rand Society of Model Engineers, 50 Golf Club Terrace, corner Louis Botha Drive and Golf Club Terrace, Florida, 082 837 2371.

Eat: Eagle's Fare Restaurant at Walter Sisulu National Botanical Garden, 082 671 8382/7, 083 414 9843.

Shop: Clearwater Mall, Hendrik Potgieter Drive and Christiaan de Wet Road, Strubens Valley, 011 288 5260.

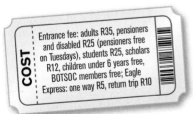

COST
Entrance fee: adults R35, pensioners and disabled R25 (pensioners free on Tuesdays), students R25, scholars R12, children under 6 years free, BOTSOC members free; Eagle Express: one way R5, return trip R10

Take note:
You are not allowed to picnic on the lawns surrounding the waterfall area, but there are numerous shady spots around the gardens where this is permitted.

Outside of Johannesburg

1 Emerald Resort and Casino

2 Pilanesberg National Park

3 Suikerbosrand Nature Reserve

4 Sun City

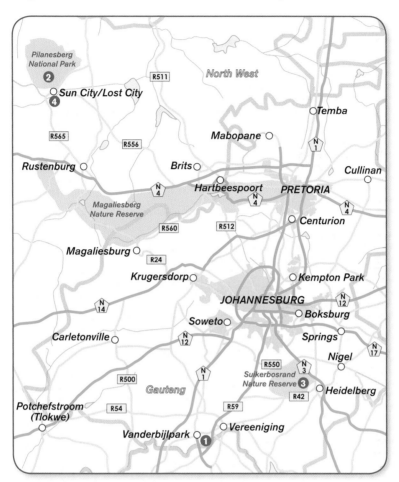

---

1 ## Emerald Resort and Casino

www.emeraldcasino.co.za

5/5 Party venue rating

5/5 Rainy day option

The resort offers an array of accommodation options, restaurants and entertainment for all ages. Animal World gives you the opportunity to view a range of birds, reptiles and land mammals, either in a zoo environment or in larger enclosures during a game drive. You can also try rock climbing, putt putt at Adventure Golf, slip 'n slide at the indoor Aquadome, bowl a strike at the Pins Bowling Alley, or play computer games and surf the internet at i-Zone. Children from four to 12 years can enjoy supervised fun at the KidZone indoor play centre and toy store. The restaurants and children's entertainment are in a separate building to the casino.

Tel number	016 982 8000
Address	777 Frikkie Meyer Boulevard, Vanderbijlpark
GPS marker	26°44'32"S; 27°51'28"E
Opening hours	Adventure Golf: 10am–5pm Monday to Sunday;
	Animal World: 9am–4:15pm Monday to Sunday;
	Aquadome: summer (1 September to 30 April) 10am–6pm Sunday to Thursday and public holidays, 10am–8pm Friday and Saturday, winter (1 May–31 August) 10am–6pm Monday to Sunday;
	i-Zone: 10am–11pm Monday to Friday, 8am–11pm Saturday, Sunday, public holidays and school holidays;
	KidZone: 8am–11pm Monday to Sunday;
	Pins Bowling Alley: 9am–6pm (day), 6pm until closing (night);
	Rock climbing: 10am–5pm Monday to Sunday;
	Casino: 10am–4am Monday to Thursday, 10am Friday to 4am Sunday
Most appropriate age group	4+
Pram/wheelchair-friendly	Yes
Baby-changing facility	Yes
Nearest hospital	Mediclinic Emfuleni, 016 950 8000
	Midvaal Private Hospital, 016 454 6000

Nearby

Eat/play/sleep: Stone Haven on Vaal, next to the Old Baddrift Bridge, Sylviavale, Vaal River, Vanderbijl-park, 016 982 2951. Bon Hotel Riviera on Vaal, Mario Milani Road, Vereeniging, 016 420 1300.

COST Free entry; Adventure Golf: R30 per person; Animal World: adults R35, pensioners R20, children R25; game drives: adults and children R40–R50, pensioners R20

Take note:
The Aquadome is heated and operates all year round. The water pumps and the water slide are only operational on weekends and on public and school holidays.

COST i-Zone: R25 per hour; KidZone: R25 per hour; Pins Bowling Al-ley: adults R40, children under 10 years and pensioners R25; rock climbing: R15 per person for two climbs

COST Aquadome summer peak rates: adults and children over 12 years R100, children under 12 years and pensioners R65, family (two adults and three children under 12 years) R350; off peak rates: adults and children over 12 years R50, children under 12 years and pensioners R40, family (two adults and three children under 12 years) R200

② Pilanesberg National Park
www.pilanesbergnationalpark.org

 2/5 Party venue rating

 5/5 Rainy day option

This semi-arid nature reserve, with nearly 200km of excellent quality roads for either self-drives or guided drives, is home to the Big Five, several other predators such as African wild dog and cheetah, and antelope such as gemsbok. The reserve is situated within the crater of an extinct volcano and surrounded by a ridge or ring of hills known as the Pilanesberg National Park Alkaline Ring Complex. There are numerous hides and scenic picnic sites within the reserve. You can purchase cold drinks, snacks and basic safari supplies at the Pilanesberg Centre that overlooks the Mankwe Dam. There is also a restaurant, toilets and an interactive computer screen with park maps and the listings of the latest sightings.

Tel number	014 555 1600
Address	Off the R556, North West Province
GPS marker	25°20'27"S; 27°03'51"E
Opening hours	Daily, March and April 6am–6:30pm, May to September 6:30am–6pm, September and October 6am–6:30pm, November to February 5:30am–7pm
Most appropriate age group	4+
Pram/wheelchair-friendly	Yes
Baby-changing facility	No
Nearest hospital	Netcare Ferncrest Hospital, 014 568 4399

Nearby
Visit/see: Airtrackers Hot Air Balloon Safaris, 014 552 5020.

COST Adults R65, pensioners R20, children R20, vehicles R20

Take note:
The reserve is situated within a malaria-free area, but it is still advisable to use mosquito repellent and mosquito nets.

3 Suikerbosrand Nature Reserve

www.suikerbos.co.za

The Suikerbosrand mountain range forms the backbone of the nature reserve. It varies in altitude between 1,545m and 1,917m above sea level. The reserve gets its name from the suikerbos or sugarbush plant, also known as the protea, which is abundant in the reserve. It is a peaceful park and a great place for mountain biking, hiking or picnicking.

Tel number	011 439 6300
Address	Off the R550/Alberton Road, Heidelberg
GPS marker	26°29'02"S; 28°13'45"E
Opening hours	7am–6pm daily; last entrance at 4pm
Most appropriate age group	7+
Pram/wheelchair-friendly	No
Baby-changing facility	No
Nearest hospital	Life Suikerbosrand Clinic, 016 342 9200

Nearby

Visit/see: Klipkerk (Stone Church), 57 HF Verwoerd Street, Lesedi Local Municipality, 016 340 4300.
Diepkloof Farmhouse Museum, Nigel Road, Lesedi Local Municipality, 016 340 4300.
Eat: The Secret Gardens, corner Jordaan and Van der Westhuizen streets, 016 341 5248.

Take note:
If you're planning on going hiking in summer, get an early start and take lots of water with you as it can get quite hot.

COST
Adults R25, children 7–17 years and pensioners R15, children 0–6 years free, R15 per vehicle

Sun City
www.suninternational.com/sun-city

4/5
Party venue rating

3/5
Rainy day option

Sun International's Sun City Resort has hundreds of activities on offer for the whole family, whether you want to spend your days driving and putting on the two world-class golf courses, viewing the Nile crocodiles at the Kwena Gardens, or cooling down at the Valley of Waves water park. The Valley of Waves has a man-made beach, numerous slides, a wave pool and lifeguards on duty daily to ensure your safety. Little ones aren't forgotten as they can attend a fun-filled activity programme at Kamp Kwena and enjoy a ride on the *Stimela* train or mini quad bikes.

Take note:
Get to the Valley of Waves early to grab a spot in the shade and take lots of sunscreen. They hire out towels and umbrellas.

Tel number	014 557 1544/3382
Address	Off the R556, North West Province
GPS marker	25°20'55"S; 27°05'59"E
Opening hours	Cable Ski: 8am–5pm daily; Kamp Kwena (4–12 years): 9am–1pm and 2pm–5pm, night care 5pm–10pm; Kwena Crèche: 10am–10pm Sunday to Thursday, 10am–11pm Friday and Saturday; Maze of the Lost City: 9am–9pm; Valley of Waves: 8am–6pm daily, closed from 1 May to 30 June; Zip line (minimum height 1.2m): 8am–5pm daily
Most appropriate age group	5+
Pram/wheelchair-friendly	Yes
Baby-changing facility	Yes
Nearest hospital	Netcare Ferncrest Hospital, 014 568 4399

Nearby

Visit/see: Pilanesberg National Park, R556, 087 820 0020. Predator World, R556, 014 552 6900.

Play/do: Segway Gliding Tours at Sun City, R556, 0861 025 327.

COST From R60 per person on arrival; babysitting service: R60 per hour; Cable Ski: beginner's lesson R1,200, R599 per person; Kamp Kwena: R95 per session; Kwena Crèche: R45 per hour

COST Maze of the Lost City: adults R100, children under 12 years R60; Valley of Waves: adults and children 13 years and older R120–R150, pensioners R60, children 4–12 years R70–R80, children under 3 years free; Zip line: R520 per person

Getting around Pretoria

Public transport in Pretoria is mainly for commuters and choices are limited for the out-of-town visitor. Most locals use their cars to get around, or use mini-bus taxis, but the latter have a reputation as dangerous, and the system they work on can be mind-boggling for a tourist. If you do travel by car, keep your windows up at all times (to prevent smash-and-grab incidents), leave all valuables out of sight and be aware of car hijackings. When you park your car, always lock it and stow valuables in the boot. There are, however, two Gautrain stations in the city (Pretoria CBD and Hatfield) and two in the southern part of the city (Midrand and Centurion). From these stations you can choose several routes for the Gautrain bus: Brooklyn, Lynnwood, Arcadia, Hatfield, Queenswood, Highveld, Rooihuiskraal, Wierda Park, Southdowns, CBD, Groenkloof, Pretoria Zoo, Randjespark, Noordwyk and Sunninghill. The Gautrain also takes you directly to OR Tambo International Airport. Just a reminder: you need to buy a prepaid Gautrain card beforehand.

Rental car companies
Avis
012 301 5020
www.avis.co.za

Bidvest Car Rental
086 101 7722
www.bidvestcarrental.co.za
Europcar
086 113 1000
www.europcar.co.za

Taxis and shuttles
Rixi Taxis
0861 00 7494
www.rixitaxi.co.za
Zebra Cabs
0861 105 105
www.zebracabs.co.za
Pretoria Shuttle
071 012 2780, 073 648 1213,
079 130 0198
www.pretoriashuttle.co.za
Shuttle Direct
0861 734 732, 012 997 6534,
012 997 5628, 079 236 7011 (after hours)
Speedy Ride
076 144 3442
www.speedyride.co.za

Gautrain
0800 428 87246
www.gautrain.co.za

Central Pretoria

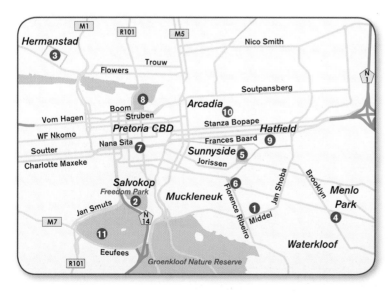

1. Austin Roberts Bird Sanctuary
2. Freedom Park
3. Friends of the Rail (FOTR) Steam Train Excursions
4. Hazel Food Market
5. Loftus Versfeld Stadium
6. Magnolia Dell Park
7. Museum Mall
8. National Zoological Gardens
9. Sci-Enza
10. Union Buildings
11. Voortrekker Monument

1 Austin Roberts Bird Sanctuary

The sanctuary has been declared a Heritage Site because of its recreational and educational value. It covers 11.8ha and is within the Walkerspruit Open Space System. Two streams feed into the wetlands, attracting over 170 bird species. Guided walks in the sanctuary can be arranged, and bird viewing is also popular – either on a guided walk or from the deck of the restaurant on the banks of the lake. There is also a children's play park.

Take note: Pack a picnic and enjoy a day at the sanctuary. Sundays are especially popular.

Tel number	012 440 8316
Address	Melk Street, Pretoria
GPS marker	25°46'14"S; 28°13'40"E
Opening hours	6am–6pm in summer, 7am–5pm in winter
Most appropriate age group	4+
Pram/wheelchair-friendly	No
Baby-changing facility	No
Nearest hospital	Little Company of Mary Hospital, 012 424 3600

Nearby
Eat: The Blue Crane Restaurant, Melk Street, Nieuw Muckleneuk, 012 460 7615. Jam and Daisies, corner Lange and Tram streets, Nieuw Muckleneuk, 012 346 6692.
Sleep: Illyria House, 327 Bourke Street, Muckleneuk, 012 344 5193. Crane's Nest Guest House, 303 Aquila Avenue, Waterkloof Ridge, 012 460 7223.

COST — Free entry; guided walks R55 (booking essential)

2 Freedom Park
www.freedompark.co.za

The park celebrates 3.6 billion years of history through an African perspective. The Freedom Park Museum – or //hapo, the Khoi word for dream – tells the story of Africa, and of South Africa specifically, in seven parts. These are earth, ancestors, peopling, resistance and colonisation, industrialisation and urbanisation, nationalism and struggle, as well as nation building and continent building. Follow the story through interactive displays, vivid audiovisual presentations, performances and storytelling. The Garden of Remembrance is the final resting place of people who gave their lives in the conflicts that shaped South Africa. The tranquil garden houses S'khumbuto, the park's main memorial; Isivivane, the boulders; and Uitspanplek.

Tel number	012 336 4000
Address	Corner 7th Avenue and Koch Street, Salvokop
GPS marker	25°45'51"S; 28°11'14"E
Opening hours	8am–4:30pm daily; guided tours take place at 9am, 1pm, 2pm and 3pm; you can book tours online
Most appropriate age group	1+
Pram/wheelchair-friendly	Yes
Baby-changing facility	Yes
Nearest hospital	Zuid Afrikaans Hospital, 012 343 0300

Take note:
Pack a picnic and enjoy a day out in the park's serene spot, Uitspanplek, with beautiful views of the city.

COST
Adults R45–R90, children 5–12 years old and pensioners R25–R70, children under 5 free

Nearby

Visit/see: Jan Cilliers Park, Broderick Street, Groenkloof. Groenkloof Nature Reserve, corner Eeufees Road and Christina de Wit Avenue, Groenkloof, 012 440 8316.
Eat: Moyo, Fountains Valley Road, Groenkloof, 012 341 5729.
For parents: Café 41, Shop 1, Bronkhorst Road, Pretoria, 012 460 5216.

Special event

On 27 April each year, South Africa celebrates Freedom Day, and Freedom Park is always part of the festivities (keep an eye on their website to see what is planned)

---

3 **Friends of the Rail (FOTR) Steam Train Excursions**

www.friendsoftherail.com

5/5 Party venue rating

4/5 Rainy day option

FOTR run frequent public vintage train trips with the Tshwane Explorer to various destinations in the vicinity of the nation's capital. They also organise trips twice a month to the quaint village of Cullinan. These take about three hours, and once you've enjoyed the scenery during the trip, you can explore the village and its diamond mining history. There are various places to have a bite to eat.

Tel number	012 767 7913, 082 098 6186
Address	152 Miechaelson Street
GPS marker	25°43'11"S; 28°09'48"E
Opening hours	Departures 8am
Most appropriate age group	1+
Pram/wheelchair-friendly	No
Baby-changing facility	No
Nearest hospital	Bougainville Private Hospital, 012 379 0264

Take note:
You can rent your own private coach on any of their regular public steam train excursions for a birthday party or private function. You can do your own catering or they can help out.

COST For Cullinan: adults R250, pensioners R200, children 13–18 years old R175, children 7–12 years old R150, children 3–6 years old R100, children under 3 free

COST Tshwane Explorer: adults R200, pensioners R170, children 13–18 years old R150, children 7–12 years old R125, children 2–6 years old R75, children under 2 free

4 Hazel Food Market
www.hazelfoodmarket.co.za

0/5 Party venue rating   **2/5** Rainy day option

You'll find anything from fresh fruit, veggies, meat, tarts and sweets to freshly baked breads, all types of ready-to-eat meals, cappuccinos, mouth-watering milkshakes, flowers, home-grown herbs, deli-style products and much more. You can stock up on eats and enjoy a picnic, while children can unwind in the play area.

Tel number	083 554 5636
Address	64 13th Street, Menlo Park
GPS marker	25°46'12"S; 28°15'27"E
Opening hours	8am–2pm every Saturday (including over long weekends and public holidays that fall on a Saturday)
Most appropriate age group	1+
Pram/wheelchair-friendly	Yes
Baby-changing facility	No
Nearest hospital	Life Faerie Glen Hospital, 012 369 5600

Nearby

Eat: Toni's Fully Furnished Pizza Co, 81 Thomas Edison St, Menlo Park, 012 346 5370, 012 346 2508. Boer'geoisie, Greenlyn Village Centre, 13th Street, Menlo Park, 012 460 0264.
Sleep: Farmers Folly Guest House, 40 Farmers Folly Road, Lynnwood, 012 348 3449.

Take note:
The market is famous for bringing you foods from around the globe, freshly made in Pretoria. Taste Indonesian cuisine, cooking from the Netherlands, Moroccan fare, Mexican treats, Armenian eats and more.

5 Loftus Versfeld Stadium
www.thebulls.co.za

Visit the stadium when the Bulls are in action, even if it's just to soak up the atmosphere. Bulls fans are as close to 'tamed fanatics' as one can get. Before matches, braai fires burn all around the stadium and fans dress in blue, many sporting hats with horns. The stadium can take almost 52,000 spectators and, if the Bulls are on a winning streak, their excitement can be heard across Pretoria. Buy some eats and souvenirs when you take the family to experience a national pastime at one of the country's best stadiums, also known as Fort Loftus. Tours of the stadium, the Bulls' locker room and the Blue Bulls Museum can be arranged by appointment.

Tel number	012 420 0700
Address	Kirkness Street, Pretoria
GPS marker	25°45'11"S; 28°13'22"E
Closest public transport	Hatfield Gautrain Station is within walking distance, and from Hatfield station the Gautrain buses H1 and H3 travel to the stadium
Most appropriate age group	4+
Pram/wheelchair-friendly	Yes
Nearest hospital	Mediclinic Medforum, 021 809 6500

COST Varies depending on tournament

Nearby
Visit/see: Melrose House, 275 Jeff Masemola Street, Pretoria Central, 012 322 2805.
Eat: The Harlequin Restaurant, 56 Totius Street, 012 460 5291.
Sleep: Oorkant Loftus Guest House, 439 Kirkness Street, 012 344 2289.

Special events
The big rugby tournaments that are sure to have matches at Loftus are international Springbok matches, Super Rugby, Currie Cup and Vodacom Cup matches

Take note: In addition to hosting rugby matches, Loftus has also been the venue for memorable soccer matches and concerts featuring international stars.

6 Magnolia Dell Park
www.facebook.com/Magnolia Dell Park

 3/5 Party venue rating
 3/5 Rainy day option

This is one of the most beautiful and popular parks in Pretoria. When the magnolia trees are in bloom around springtime, the park is the perfect place to meet with friends and enjoy the outdoors. Walker Spruit runs through the park and it's the ideal picnic spot, with jungle gyms to entertain children. Well-behaved dogs are also welcome. On the last Saturday of every month the Magnolia Dell Art in the Park takes place (10am–3pm). On the first Saturday of the month the Magnolia Dell Craft Market runs from 9am to 2pm, and on some Friday evenings the Moonlight Market is open from 5:30pm to 9:30pm.

Address	Corner Florence Ribeiro Avenue and University Road, Hatfield
GPS marker	25°45'41"S; 28°13'11"E
Closest public transport	Gautrain bus route H1 Hatfield
Most appropriate age group	1+
Pram/wheelchair-friendly	Yes
Baby-changing facility	Yes
Nearest hospital	Zuid Afrikaans Hospital, 012 343 0300

Nearby
Eat: Blue Crane Restaurant, Melk Street, Pretoria, 012 460 7615. Huckleberries, Florence Ribeiro Avenue, 012 346 4588.
Shop/visit: Brooklyn Mall, Bronkhorst Street, Pretoria, 012 346 1063. Brooklyn Design Fair, Brooklyn Square, level 2, corner Middel and Veale streets, Nieuw Muckleneuk, 082 582 8837.
Sleep: Cascades Guest House, 174 Premier Street, Waterkloof, 012 452 9980.

Take note:
South Africa's first ever love lock bridge is in Magnolia Dell Park. Here lovers lock a padlock on the bridge and throw away the key, thus locking their love forever. Other famous love lock bridges include Pont des Arts in Paris and a few bridges over the Yarra River in Melbourne, Australia.

Special event
On selected Fridays the locals gather to buy crafts at the Magnolia Dell Moonlight Market, the perfect place to shop for an authentic souvenir; consult their Facebook page for dates

7 Museum Mall

www.ditsong.org.za

 0/5 Party venue rating
 3/5 Rainy day option

The area around the Museum of Natural History in the Pretoria CBD is the largest focal point of cultural resources in Africa. It includes tourist attractions, historical buildings and museums. Paved walkways have signs directing you to the museums. These include Melrose House, a stately mansion built in 1886; Burgers Park, established in 1870 and declared a South African national monument; Pretoria City Hall; the Children's Museum; the Ditsong National Museum of Natural History (formerly the Transvaal Museum); the National Museum of Cultural History; the Museum of Science and Technology; and the State Library. Each museum has its own secure parking, or you can make use of the walkways on a clear day.

Tel numbers	Melrose House: 012 322 2805
	Museum of Science and Technology: 012 322 6404
	Ditsong National Museum of Natural History: 012 322 7632, 012 000 0040
	National Museum of Cultural History: 012 324 6082
	State Library: 012 401 9700
Addresses	Melrose House: 275 Jeff Masemola Street
	Museum of Science and Technology: 211 Nana Sita Street
	Ditsong National Museum of Natural History: 432 Paul Kruger Street
	National Museum of Cultural History: 149 Visagie Street
	State Library: 239 Madiba Street
	Burgers Park: Burgers Park Avenue
	Pretoria City Hall: Paul Kruger Street
GPS markers	Melrose House: 25°45'20"S; 28°11'33"E
	Museum of Science and Technology: 25°45'10"S; 28°11'06"E
	Ditsong National Museum of Natural History: 25°45'12"S; 28°11'20"E
	National Museum of Cultural History: 25°45'12"S; 28°11'04"E
	State Library: 25°44'42"S; 28°11'23"E
	Burgers Park: 25°45'16"S; 28°11'33"E
Closest public transport	Gautrain bus stations: Pretoria Station or Bosman Street Station
Opening hours	Melrose House: 10am–5pm Tuesday to Sunday
	Ditsong National Museum of Natural History: 8am–4pm daily
	National Museum of Cultural History: 8am–4pm daily
	Museum of Science and Technology: 8am–4pm Monday to Friday, 2pm–5pm Saturday
	State Library: 8:30am–6pm Monday, Tuesday, Thursday and Friday, 9:30am–6pm Wednesday, 8:30am–4pm Saturday
Most appropriate age group	6+
Pram/wheelchair-friendly	Yes
Baby-changing facility	No
Nearest hospital	Medforum Private Hospital, 012 317 6700

Nearby

Visit/see: Church Square or Kruger House Museum, Church Street, 012 326 9172.

COST

Melrose House: adults R8, children R5, guided tours R50 plus entrance fee; Burgers Park: free; Pretoria City Hall: free

COST

Ditsong National Museum of Natural History: senior citizens R10, learners R15, guided tours for learners R20; Discovery Centre: R20, adults R30, guided tours for adults R35, behind the scenes tour R50

COST

National Museum of Cultural History: children and pensioners R20, adults R35; Museum of Science and Technology: R25; State Library: free

Take note:
Tshwane Metro Council is planning on fencing off the Museum Mall area for extra security. When you do explore this area, please be extra careful with belongings.

(8) National Zoological Gardens

www.nzg.ac.za

5/5 Party venue rating

3/5 Rainy day option

This South African gem has got plenty to offer visitors. You can book either of the two tours: camping – spend the night as a family in the zoo; and night tours – meet the nocturnal residents of the zoo. On daily visits to the 84ha zoo you can expect to see about 5,000 different mammals, birds, fish, reptiles, amphibians and invertebrates, comprising around 600 species and subspecies. The zoo also boasts the largest inland aquarium in Africa and it's the only South African zoo where you can see koalas, okapi, komodo dragons and forest buffalo. The zoo offers various educational programmes for children, as well as regular events. Also visit the cableway for spectacular views and the restaurants for something to eat.

Tel number	012 339 2700
Address	232 Boom Street, Pretoria Central
GPS marker	25°44'21"S; 28°11'20"E
Closest public transport	The Gautrain bus, which departs from the Gautrain Pretoria Station (adjacent to the existing Pretoria Main Station), stops at the zoo
Opening hours	8:30am–5:30pm daily (last tickets sold at 4:30pm); cable car: 10am–4:15pm
Most appropriate age group	1+
Pram/wheelchair-friendly	Yes
Baby-changing facility	Yes
Nearest hospital	Tshwane District Hospital, 012 354 5958

Take note:
You can get involved with the zoo by 'becoming their friend', joining the Zoo Club or adopting a Wild Child.

Nearby
Visit/see: South African State Theatre, 320 Pretorius Street, 012 392 4000.

Special event
On Heritage Day, 24 September, the zoo organises something special to celebrate our cultural heritage and its diversity, as well as our immense natural wealth (it's also known as Braai Day, so the zoo makes provision for family braais near the Apies River that runs through the venue)

COST: Cable car: adults R20 one-way and R30 return, children R15 one-way and R20 return, school groups R15 per person

COST: The entrance fee includes a visit to the Aquarium and Reptile Park, as well as the zoo: adults R85, children 2–15 years old R55, R35 per person in an educational group (only Monday to Wednesday), R50 per person in an educational group (Thursday and Friday)

9 Sci-Enza
www.up.ac.za

This is the oldest interactive science centre in South Africa. A must-see is the Camera Obscura on the roof of the Natural Science building. This is actually a dark room where the pin-hole principle of cameras is used, along with more sophisticated mirrors and lenses to allow you to have a spectacular view of the city. You actually stand inside a large camera viewing the world. Visit the centre to examine, discover, explore and enjoy science.

Tel number	012 420 2865, 012 420 3767
Address	Prosper Street, University of Pretoria
GPS marker	25°45'08"S; 28°13'53"E
Closest public transport	Gautrain Hatfield Station
Opening hours	On booking only
Most appropriate age group	5+
Pram/wheelchair-friendly	Yes
Baby-changing facility	No
Nearest hospital	Mediclinic Muelmed, 012 440 0600

COST Group bookings R10, technology workshops R15

Nearby
Visit/see: Springbok Park, between Hilda and Grosvenor streets.
Shop: Duncan Yard, Jan Shoba Street, Hatfield.
Eat: Deli on Duncan, Jan Shoba Street, Hatfield, 012 362 4054.
Hatfield Dros, corner Pretorius and Grosvenor streets, 012 430 3449.

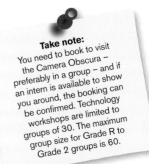

Take note:
You need to book to visit the Camera Obscura – preferably in a group – and if an intern is available to show you around, the booking can be confirmed. Technology workshops are limited to groups of 30. The maximum group size for Grade R to Grade 2 groups is 60.

---

10 Union Buildings
www.thepresidency.gov.za

The official seat of South Africa's government is built on Meintjieskop, the highest point of South Africa's capital city. The Union Buildings also house the Presidency and the Department of International Relations and Cooperation. The buildings are considered an archi-tectural masterpiece, but unfortunately they are not open to the public. The terraced indigenous gardens, though, are very popular for picnics and feature various monuments depicting the history of the country. The centrepiece is a 9m bronze statue of Nelson Mandela. Other statues include General Louis Botha, the first prime minister of the Union of South Africa, and former prime minister Barry Hertzog.

Tel number	012 300 5200
Address	Government Avenue
GPS marker	25°44'26"S; 28°12'43"E
Closest public transport	Gautrain Bus, H3 Route Arcadia
Opening hours	5am–11pm daily
Most appropriate age group	3+
Pram/wheelchair-friendly	Yes
Baby-changing facility	No
Nearest hospital	Medforum Private Hospital, 012 317 6700

Take note:
During the day there are arts and crafts for sale next to the parking area, and there are public toilets.

Nearby
Visit/see: Pretoria Art Museum, corner Frances Baard and Wessels streets, Arcadia Park, 012 344 1807.
Play/do: Venning Park Rosarium, Frances Baard Road, 012 343 3344.
Eat: Harrie's Pancakes, Eastwood Village Shopping Centre, Pretorius Street, Arcadia, 012 342 3613.
Rosies Restaurant, Venning Park, 082 641 2054.

Special event
On 9 August 1956, 20,000 women of all races marched to the Union Buildings to present a petition to the prime minister against the carrying of passes by women; today this famous women's march is celebrated every year on National Women's Day (9 August), with events near and at the Union Buildings

---

11 Voortrekker Monument
www.vtm.org.za

4/5 Party venue rating

4/5 Rainy day option

The majestic monument, which is set in a nature reserve, commemorates the pioneer history of South Africa as well as the history of the Afrikaner. You can take guided tours of the museum, which is now rated as one of the top 10 must-see attractions in South Africa. You can also go on a game drive, jog or cycle through the reserve and spot several species of antelope including wildebeest. There are running, cycling and hiking trails. Other outdoor activities include bird watching and horse riding. There are two restaurants and a tea garden on the premises, as well as a kiosk, complete with a jumping castle to keep little ones busy. The Sunday buffet is very popular.

Take note:
Apart from the Voortrekker Monument itself, there are about 11 other attractions at this venue, including a heritage centre, the Wall of Remembrance, Fort Schanskop and the Communion Wagon.

COST

Entrance to site R15–R80;
hiking, jogging or cycling
R35; entrance to monuments
and museums R30–R120
(guide R300)

Tel number	012 326 6770, 012 325 7885, 012 325 0477
Address	Eufees Road, Groenkloof
GPS marker	25°46'35"S; 28°10'33"E
Opening hours	8am–5pm 1 May to 31 August, 8am–6pm 1 September to 30 April
Most appropriate age group	5+
Pram/wheelchair-friendly	Yes
Baby-changing facility	No
Nearest hospital	Zuid Afrikaans Hospital, 012 343 0300

Nearby
Visit/see: Fort Klapperkop, Eeufees Road, Groenkloof, 012 326 6770.

Northern Pretoria

1 K1 Racing
2 Ludwig's Roses

3 Roodeplaat Nature Reserve
4 Wonderboom Nature Reserve

1 K1 Racing
www.k1racing.co.za

5/5 Party venue rating

5/5 Rainy day option

Have a race against friends with indoor go-karting. The track has a timing system, so you can race each other. Opt for the arrive-and-drive package to quickly settle adrenaline urges, or enter the grand prix. They also offer endurance races. There's a kiosk on the premises for snacks, and a television so you don't miss important sporting events.

Take note:
They are in the under-cover parking area of the Kolonnade Shopping Centre, so you can combine everything else offered at the mall with a day of racing.

Tel number	082 929 0411, 082 938 8446, 079 371 7677
Address	Kolonnade Shopping Centre, Sefako Makgatho Drive (previously Zambesi Drive), Montana Park
GPS marker	25°40'51"S; 28°15'03"E
Opening hours	Out of season: 2pm till late Tuesday to Friday, 10am till late Saturday and Sunday; in season (government school holidays) and public holidays: 10am till late daily
Most appropriate age group	6+
Pram/wheelchair-friendly	No
Baby-changing facility	No
Nearest hospital	Netcare Montana, 012 523 3000

Nearby
<u>Visit/see</u>: Montana Family Market, corner Sefako Makgatho Drive and Enkeldoorn Avenue, Montana, 012 548 6214.
<u>Play/do</u>: Mega Magic Company (tenpin bowling), Kolonnade Shopping Centre, Sefako Makgatho Drive, Montana Park, 012 548 5492/3.
<u>Eat</u>: Adega Restaurant Montana, corner Sefako Makgatho Drive and Van der Merwe Street, Montana, 012 548 3904.
<u>Shop</u>: Kolonnade Shopping Centre, Sefako Makgatho Drive, Montana Park, 012 548 1902.
<u>For parents</u>: Viva Bingo, Kolonnade Shopping Centre, Sefako Makgatho Drive, Montana Park, 012 548 1228.

Special event
The Montana Family Market (open 9am–5pm Tuesday to Sunday and public holidays) has more than 500 stalls and two play parks on site for children; there are live shows every weekend and on public holidays when some of South Africa's

COST
Arrive and drive: 10 laps R60, 20 laps R80, 30 laps R100, 50 laps R150, 3-in-1 special (15 + 20 + 30 laps) R210 per driver; grand prix: 100 laps R250 per driver; endurance races: 30 minutes R300 per kart, 1 hour R600 per kart, 90 minutes R860 per kart

2 Ludwig's Roses

www.ludwigsroses.co.za

 5/5 Party venue rating

 4/5 Rainy day option

Walk among roses and buy rose-related products from Thorns 'n Things. There is also a bird-watching station, ample space for children to play, and a butterfly garden. The farm runs regular workshops for children to learn more about potting, for example. There are Easter egg hunts and seasonal festivals. Be sure to visit the restaurant too.

Take note:
The seasonal festivities at the farm usually include tractor rides through the roses, a children's playground and a rose-themed menu at the restaurant.

Tel number	012 544 0144
Address	N1 Polokwane highway, Wallmannsthal/Pyramid off-ramp no. 163
GPS marker	25°34'36"S; 28°17'17"E
Opening hours	8am–5pm daily
Most appropriate age group	1+
Pram/wheelchair-friendly	Yes
Baby-changing facility	Yes
Nearest hospital	Netcare Montana, 012 523 3000

Nearby
Eat: Spiced Coffee Restaurant, on Ludwig's Rose Farm, 012 544 0144.
Sleep: Hoffanhein Lodge, Plot 17, Ribbok Street, Waterval, 012 545 7904.

Special event
The farm also runs the Azalea Festival each year (visit their website for more details)

3 Roodeplaat Nature Reserve

www.roodeplaat-reserve.co.za

 2/5 Party venue rating

 1/5 Rainy day option

Roodeplaat Dam is a well-known destination for bird watching, game viewing and a range of water sports including freshwater angling. The southern side of the reserve is popular with bird watchers and wildlife enthusiasts. There's a hiking trail, picnic area and overnight chalets. The northern side of the reserve is for adrenaline junkies and those with water-sports equipment. There are also camping facilities.

Tel number	012 808 5086
Address	Off the R573, Roodeplaat
GPS marker	25°37'26"S; 28°20'45"E
Opening hours	Northern side 6am–8pm, southern side 6am–6pm
Most appropriate age group	4+
Pram/wheelchair-friendly	No
Baby-changing facility	No
Nearest hospital	Montana Private Hospital, 012 523 3000

Take note:
Pack a picnic. There are tables under shady trees.

Nearby

Play/do: Rocky Ridge Estate, Mooipoort Street, Kameeldrift-East, 082 566 6360.

Eat: The Blades, Kameeldrift Road, Kameeldrift, 012 808 9943. Papachinos Silver Lakes, corner Lynnwood and Silver Lakes roads, 012 809 3539.

Sleep: Gabbata Lodge, Stand 69/70 Leeufontein, Kameelfontein, 082 468 0393. Intundla Game Lodge, Portion 7 Hammanskraal Road (R628), Dinokeng, 012 735 9913.

4 Wonderboom Nature Reserve

5/5 Party venue rating

0/5 Rainy day option

This reserve holds many significant sites such as the trunk of the Wonderboom (Miracle tree), a fig tree believed to be over 1,000 years old that was 55m wide and 25m tall. Legend has it that a chief of an indigenous tribe lies buried beneath it, causing it to grow so big. Archeologically, the reserve is home to both an Iron Age and a Stone Age excavation site. You can take walks in the reserve and see a variety of birdlife and wildlife, including guinea fowl, dassies, antelope and Verreaux's eagles.

COST Adults R31, children 7–12 years old R19, children younger than 6 R11, pensioners and the disabled R20; guided day hikes R60, guides R160

Tel number	012 543 0918
Address	On the M1, Wonderboom
GPS marker	25°41'20"S; 28°11'23"E
Opening hours	7am–6pm; no entry after 4pm
Most appropriate age group	5+
Pram/wheelchair-friendly	Yes
Baby-changing facility	No
Nearest hospital	Intercare Wonderboom, 012 543 4000

Take note:
The reserve has picnic facilities.

Nearby
<u>Eat</u>: Villa San Giovanni, Wonderboom Airport main terminal building, Linvelt Road, Wonderboom, 012 543 0501. (They have facilities for children's parties.)

Pretoria East

1. 19-Hole Putt Putt
2. Cedar Junction Theme Park
3. Faerie Glen Municipal Nature Reserve
4. Market @ The Collection
5. Pretoria Boeremark
6. Pretoria National Botanical Garden
7. Safari Garden Centre
8. Sammy Marks Museum
9. The Climbing Barn
10. The Farm Inn
11. Wolwespruit Mountain Bike and Trail Park
12. Zita Park

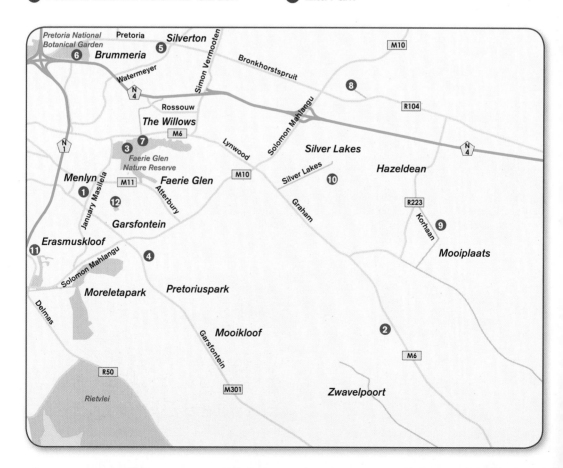

1 19-Hole Putt Putt

www.onestopentertainment.co.za

They have two 18-hole putt putt courses beneath the trees and close to a tea garden, the Waffle House, the kiosk and a relaxing area with games such as dominoes, chess or fingerboard. For parties there is a mini town consisting of a hospital, snack bar, boutique, church and more, and a play area with a mini house and jungle gym.

Tel number	072 720 6321, 082 463 2029, 072 720 6321
Address	Corner January Masilela Drive (formerly General Louis Botha Avenue) and Serene Street, Menlyn
GPS marker	25°47'22"S; 28°16'58"E
Opening hours	9am–5pm Tuesday to Thursday, 9am–6pm Friday to Sunday
Most appropriate age group	1+
Pram/wheelchair-friendly	Yes
Baby-changing facility	No
Nearest hospital	Life Faerie Glen Hospital, 012 369 5600

Nearby
Visit/see: Capital Urban Market, 170 Corobay Avenue, www.marketcapital.co.za
Eat: Panarotti's Pizza Pasta Menlyn, corner Atterbury Road and Lois Avenue, shop UF 17 and 18, Menlyn Shopping Centre, 012 368 1744.
Shop: Menlyn Park, corner Atterbury Road and Lois Avenue, Menlyn Park, 012 471 0600.

Take note:
Their party venues cater for children from one to five years old, with a separate area for children from the age of six and older.

COST: Putt putt: R45 for three rounds of 18 holes each valid for one month; party options vary

② Cedar Junction Theme Park
www.cedarjunction.co.za

5/5 Party venue rating

2/5 Rainy day option

Zwavelpoort

M6

This is an all-in-one fun park and party venue offering mini train rides, a zip line, pedal boats on the lake, a jungle gym with a sandpit, a jumping castle, a toddler play area, a trampoline and swimming pool with a slide, all in a safe, secure environment. There is a tuck shop on a timber deck overlooking the lake. There is also animal viewing.

Take note: Children are welcome to bring their own bicycles to the venue. There is a mini bike track.

COST
R20 per person Wednesday to Friday, adults R20 Saturday and Sunday, children R30 Saturday and Sunday (entry for jungle gyms, swimming pool with slide, trampoline, jumping castles and viewing of animals)

COST
Additional costs: train rides R10 per ride, pony rides R10 per ride, zip line R30 per slide, and pedal boats R50 per boat (takes four)

Tel number	012 811 1183, 082 766 2748
Address	Plot 404, Graham Road, Zwavelpoort
GPS marker	25°50'10"S; 28°23'45"E
Opening hours	8am–4:30pm Wednesday to Sunday
Most appropriate age group	1+
Pram/wheelchair-friendly	Yes
Baby-changing facility	Yes
Nearest hospital	Wilgers Hospital, 012 807 8100

Nearby

Play/do: Graceland Fun Farm, Plot 198, Zwavelpoort, 081 043 2990.
Eat: Bronberg Wynlandgoed, Plot 49, corner Graham and Boschkop roads, Zwavelpoort, 076 452 6182.

Special event

Twice a year (around March/April and September/October) the Tierlantynkies Kuier en Koop Fees (56 Saal Street, Zwavelpoort, www.tierlantynkies.co.za) takes place. More than 70 exhibitors sell a variety of goods, including jewellery, gifts, toys, clothing, leather goods and décor items, and there are many food and deli stalls offering delicious treats. You can enjoy a meal, and a glass of wine, while being entertained by local musicians, and for the children there are creative workshops, cupcake decorating, Lego competitions, face painting and more.

3 Faerie Glen Municipal Nature Reserve

 0/5 Party venue rating

 3/5 Rainy day option

This is a 128ha oasis in the middle of suburbia, with idyllic scenery, nature walks and more than 150 bird species. You will be able to spot South Africa's national flower, the protea, growing on the hillside, as well as small mammals such as mongooses, hedgehogs, hares and others. The reserve forms part of the Moreleta Spruit Nature Trail; the Moreleta Spruit flows through it, resulting in rich vegetation. There are numerous hiking trails, varying in difficulty. You can also take your dog along, as long as it is kept on a leash.

Tel number	012 358 1510
Address	January Masilela Avenue, Faerie Glen
GPS marker	25°46'28"S; 28°17'43"E
Opening hours	6am–6pm
Most appropriate age group	3+
Pram/wheelchair-friendly	Yes
Baby-changing facility	No
Nearest hospital	Life Faerie Glen Hospital, 012 369 5600

Nearby

Visit/see: Art @ Boardwalk, corner Solomon Mahlangu Drive and Haymeadow Crescent, Faerie Glen, 074 193 0094.

Play/do: Anja's Tea Garden, 6 Koedoeberg Road, Faerie Glen, 072 153 6732.

Eat: Steak Inn Grill & Butcher, corner Hans Strydom Drive and Haymeadow Crescent, 012 991 4733. Plumbago Tea Garden, entrance of Faerie Glen Nature Reserve. Taste Life Café, 66A Olympus Drive, 083 276 4658.

Shop: Glen Village Shopping Centre, corner Hans Strydom and Olympus drives, Faerie Glen, 012 992 6103.

For parents: Nuvo Cuisine, 823 Old Farm Road, 012 991 3396.

Take note:
There are no facilities in the reserve and it's advised not to explore it alone.

COST Children 0–6 years old free, adults R6, pensioners R3

4 Market @ The Collection

www.thecollection.co.za

 5/5 Party venue rating
 0/5 Rainy day option

This evening market has a rare offering: mini and vintage cars and a train collection are on display. With this nostalgic backdrop you can shop for speciality eats (the pizzas are very popular), and visit the bistro with a fully licensed bar. There is live music, craft stalls and loads of entertainment for the children.

Tel number	012 993 3638
Address	5 Boendoe Road, off Garsfontein Drive, Pretoria East
GPS marker	25°46'04"S; 28°24'38"E
Opening hours	4pm–8pm every Friday
Most appropriate age group	1+
Pram/wheelchair-friendly	Yes
Baby-changing facility	No
Nearest hospital	Netcare Pretoria East Hospital, 012 422 2300

COST: Adults R20, children free entry

Take note:
The Collection also hosts children's birthday parties in a beautiful garden setting, with ponds, ducks and an open garden area.

Nearby

Visit/see: Barnyard Theatre Parkview, 1 Garsfontein Road, Parkview, 012 368 1555.
Play/do: Moreleta Kloof Nature Reserve, Blouhaak and Rutgers avenues, Moreleta Park. Jingle Jangle, Wekker Street, Moreleta Park, 012 997 0134.
Eat: Antonnio's Italian Kitchen, Shop 27, Parkview Lifestyle Centre, Moreleta Park, 012 992 6111. Die Bos, 124 Wekker Road, Moreleta Park, 079 777 6125.
Ciao! Restaurant, The Village, 1220 Wekker Road, 012 997 0323.

5 Pretoria Boeremark

www.pretoriaboeremark.co.za

 0/5 Party venue rating
 1/5 Rainy day option

Very early on Saturday mornings the grounds of the Pioneer Museum come alive when vendors start setting up stalls with fresh fruit, vegetables, meat, baked breads, arts and crafts, and more. After shopping it's time to indulge in 'Boere' fare with roosterkoek, vetkoek, pannekoek, koeksisters, jaffels, pap, kaiings, coffee and more. Enjoy your eats at the dam and watch the ducks and geese.

Tel number	012 804 8031, 079 987 1025
Address	Pioneer Museum, Keuning Drive, Silverton
GPS marker	25°44'07"S; 28°18'34"E
Opening hours	4:30am–10am Saturday
Most appropriate age group	4+
Pram/wheelchair-friendly	Yes
Baby-changing facility	No
Nearest hospital	Silverton Clinic, 012 804 8958

Nearby
Visit/see: Pioneer Museum, Struben Street, 012 813 8006, 072 323 9758.

Take note:
The market does not run on Saturdays if it's a Christian holiday.

---

6 Pretoria National Botanical Garden
www.sanbi.org/gardens/pretoria

This is a 76ha urban oasis divided into two sections by a quartzite outcrop. This means visitors can experience two different botanical worlds – the colder south side and the warmer north side. Some 50ha of the garden is dedicated to an indigenous garden, with almost half of the country's tree species on display. Other plant species indigenous to South Africa, but not endemic to this area, such as fynbos and forests, can also be viewed here. Paved walkways allow visitors to see all the areas in the garden and you may be able to spot any of the more than 200 bird species, reptiles and small mammals to be found here. The Eco Craft Gift Shop is also on the premises.

Take note:
No cycling, ball sports, open fires, loud music, tree climbing, flower picking, swimming or pets are allowed.

Tel number	012 843 5172
Address	2 Cussonia Avenue, Pretoria East
GPS marker	28°16'20"S; 25°44'18"E
Opening hours	8am–6pm daily (no entry after 5pm); shop: 9am–5pm Monday to Friday, 10am–5pm Saturday, 1pm–5pm Sunday
Most appropriate age group	1+
Pram/wheelchair-friendly	Yes
Baby-changing facility	Yes
Nearest hospital	Medicross Silverton, 012 845 1300

COST
Adults R26, students R16, children R12, children under 6 years old free, SA senior citizens (with ID) free on Tuesdays, BOTSOC members free

Nearby

Play/do: Supersport United Soccer Schools, 627 Meiring Naudé Drive, Brummeria, 079 254 9355.
Eat: Mokha Restaurant, 2 Cussonia Ave, 012 804 1714.
Sleep: The Bushbaby Inn, 11 Suikerbos Drive, 012 804 9239.
For parents: Casa Toscana Lodge and Die Blou Hond Theatre, 5 Darling Road, 012 348 8820.

Special event

Every other Sunday afternoon from May to September the Old Mutual Music in the Gardens series takes place at the park, where local musicians perform in an idyllic setting among the plants. Pack a picnic, take the whole family and enjoy music in nature.

---

7 Safari Garden Centre
www.safarigardencentre.com

4/5 Party venue rating

1/5 Rainy day option

This nursery is a multi-award-winning garden centre where you can buy plants, get advice and allow the children to run wild in the fresh air. They can enjoy pony rides and the Safari Fun Train on weekends. There is a huge jungle gym and enclosed play area where they can see marmoset monkeys, pot-bellied pigs, dwarf mountain goats, rabbits and more.

Tel number	012 807 0009, 012 807 4545
Address	Corner Lynnwood Road and Rubida Street, The Willows
GPS marker	25°46'02"S; 28°18'09"E
Opening hours	8am–5:30pm Monday to Saturday, 9am–5:30pm Sunday and public holidays
Most appropriate age group	4+
Pram/wheelchair-friendly	No
Baby-changing facility	No
Nearest hospital	Wilgers Hospital, 012 807 8100

Nearby

Eat: Stephnie's, Shop 7, Lynnwood Bridge Retail, corner Daventry and Lynnwood roads, 012 348 8943.

Take note:
There is a restaurant on the premises with different decks, so you can choose your view.

8 Sammy Marks Museum
www.ditsong.org.za

Sammy Marks was one of the first entrepreneurs in South Africa, playing a significant role in mining, industrial and agricultural development in this country. Marks and his family lived at Zwartkoppies Hall, the Victorian mansion that has since become the Sammy Marks Museum. The last Marks lived here until 1978. The museum was opened in 1986. There is a tea garden and restaurant.

Tel number	012 755 9542
Address	Old Bronkhorstspruit Road, Donkerhoek
GPS marker	25°44'59"S; 28°22'48"E
Opening hours	9am–5pm daily
Most appropriate age group	7+
Pram/wheelchair-friendly	No
Baby-changing facility	No
Nearest hospital	Wilgers Hospital, 012 807 8100

Nearby
Visit/see: Bester Bird and Animal Zoo Park, 44 Simon Vermooten Road, Meyerspark, 012 807 4192.
Play/do: Kinderland Party Venue, Meerlust Road, Equestria, 012 807 3157.
Eat: Afro-Boer, 1 Meerlust Avenue, corner Lynnwood Road and Meerlust Avenue, The Willows, 012 807 3099. La Vie Lente, 242 Lynnwood Road, 072 916 7801.
Shop: The Grove Mall, corner Simon Vermooten and Lynnwood roads, Equestria, 012 807 0951.
Sleep: The Willows Country Lodge, Plot 21, Lynnwood Road, The Willows, 012 807 4100.

Special event
Every year the museum celebrates Sammy Marks' birthday on 12 July. This usually includes horse-and-cart rides, face painting, food and craft stalls, veteran cars, whisky tasting, live music and more.

Take note: On certain days the museum offers ghost evenings and Victorian picnics, and bird walks in February, May and November.

COST Adults R45, pensioners and students R25, learners R15

⑨ The Climbing Barn
www.climbingbarn.co.za

 5/5 Party venue rating

 5/5 Rainy day option

This is the only climbing barn in Pretoria and caters for experienced climbers as well as beginners. There are experts on hand to help you learn the ropes. There are 160m^2 of climbing walls, including an 8m roof, 80m^2 of bouldering cave, 1,851 grips, and various routes.

Tel number	082 335 3220
Address	Korhaan Road, off Boschkop Road (M6), Mooiplaats
GPS marker	25°46'04"S; 28°24'38"E
Opening hours	4pm–9pm Monday to Friday, 10am–8pm Saturday, 10am–6pm Sunday and public holidays
Most appropriate age group	6+
Pram/wheelchair-friendly	No
Baby-changing facility	No
Nearest hospital	Intercare Sub-acute and Day Hospital, 012 880 0700

Take note:
Wear comfortable clothes when climbing and bouldering. No skirts and dresses.

Nearby
Play/do: Rosemary Hill MTB Trail, 257 Mooiplaats, N4, East exit 18, 012 802 0052.
Pro Paintball, Olivenhoutsbosch Road, Rooihuiskraal, 082 381 0574.
Eat: Tin Roof Café, off the R223, Korhaan Road, Mooiplaats, 072 367 5698.

COST: Day pass: adults R70, students R65, scholars R60; bouldering: R40; gear hire: rope R25, shoes R15, chalk bag R5, harness R20

⑩ The Farm Inn
www.farminn.co.za

 5/5 Party venue rating 3/5 Rainy day option

This is a privately owned, up-market country hotel and conference centre that offers accommodation (from luxury to self-catering), game drives, restaurants, a tea garden with a play area for children, a sculpture garden where art pieces are for sale, and an African art shop. Sunday lunch and breakfasts are very popular. They also offer children's birthday parties, which include game drives, and interaction with lion, tiger and cheetah cubs if available.

Take note:
Animal interaction with lion cubs depends on whether cubs are available. Enquire beforehand.

COST: Game drives R130 per adult, breakfast buffet R135 per adult, breakfast and game drive combo R205 per adult, Sunday lunch R195 per adult, lunch and game drive R270 per adult, cub interaction R700 for 15 minutes for groups of up to five maximum, cub interaction R100 for 10 minutes per person; children under 12 years old pay half-price of all above costs, and children under 4 years old are free

Tel number	012 809 0266, 012 809 0277, 083 252 8588
Address	Silver Lakes Road, Silver Lakes
GPS marker	25°46'59"S; 28°10'62"E
Opening hours	7am till late
Most appropriate age group	1+
Pram/wheelchair-friendly	Yes
Baby-changing facility	Yes
Nearest hospital	Intercare Silver Lakes, 012 809 6000

Nearby

Visit/see: Tuscan BBQ Buffet Restaurant and Party Venue, Plot 1, Shere Holdings, corner Lynnwood Drive and Dudley Road, Pretoria East, 012 809 0906.

Eat: Silverlakes Dros, Von Backstrom Street, Silver Lakes, 012 809 1598. Mo-Zam-Bik Restaurant, corner N4 and Solomon Maghlangu Drive, Silver Lakes, 012 817 2014.

Sleep: Sherewood Lodge, 100 Cole Road, Silver Lakes, 012 809 2398.

For parents: Silver Lakes Golf Estate, 36 La Quinta Street, Silver Lakes, 012 809 0281.

---

11 Wolwespruit Mountain Bike and Trail Park

www.wolwespruit.co.za

0/5 Party venue rating

0/5 Rainy day option

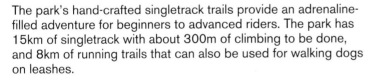

The park's hand-crafted singletrack trails provide an adrenaline-filled adventure for beginners to advanced riders. The park has 15km of singletrack with about 300m of climbing to be done, and 8km of running trails that can also be used for walking dogs on leashes.

Take note:
If you don't buy a ticket, you are not allowed to ride or run the trails. There is a tuck shop on the premises.

COST: R30 entry

Tel number	012 661 1661, 081 316 7720
Address	501 Jochemus Street, Erasmuskloof
GPS marker	25°48'37"S; 28°15'49"E
Opening hours	5:30am–9am and 4pm–6:30pm Monday, Wednesday, Thursday and Friday; 5:30am–9am and 4pm–9pm Tuesday; 6am–6pm Saturday; 7am–6pm Sunday
Most appropriate age group	5+
Pram/wheelchair-friendly	No
Baby-changing facility	No
Nearest hospital	Mediclinic Kloof, 012 367 4000

Nearby

Visit/see: Snyman Sjokelateur, 509 Gariep Street, 012 347 1828.
Play/do: Gotcha Paintball, 95 Zinnia Avenue, 086 146 8242.
Eat: Ritrovo Ristorante, 103 Club Avenue, 012 460 4367. Belle's Pretoria, The Club Shopping Centre, corner Pinaster Avenue and 18th Street, Hazelwood, 012 346 3874.
Sleep: Cascades Guest House, 174 Premier Street, 012 452 9980.

---

12 Zita Park

The park is a central point for doing quintessentially South African out-doorsy things. There is a splash pool with a relatively steep, own-risk slide, as well as a paddle pool for the little ones. Pack Frisbees and bats and balls for a game of backyard cricket. You can ride your bike or fly a kite, pack a picnic or enjoy a braai. There is plenty of space for children to run, tumble and dive. The park has ablution facilities and there is a tuck shop for energy-sapped children.

Tel number	082 528 6767
Address	Corner Zita and Len Brown streets, Garsfontein
GPS marker	25°47'33"S; 28°17'35"E
Opening hours	9am–6pm daily; pool is closed during winter (April to August)
Most appropriate age group	1+
Pram/wheelchair-friendly	No
Baby-changing facility	No
Nearest hospital	Life Faerie Glen Hospital, 012 369 5600

Nearby

Play/do: Klitsgras Drumming, Garsfontein Road, 083 311 0025. Kleinplasie, Plot 16, Midas Avenue, 072 362 0146.

Eat: Blos Café, 66A Olympus Drive, Olympus, 082 466 2857.

Shop: Waterglen Shopping Centre, corner Garsfontein Road and General Louis Botha Avenue, Waterkloof Glen.

Take note:
The Zita Park Family Café and Pizzeria is on the premises. The pizzeria is fully licensed, and children can build their own pizza.

Centurion Area

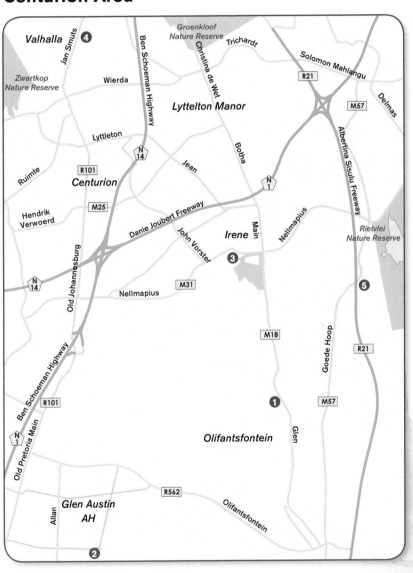

1. Acrobranch
2. Glen Austin Bird Sanctuary
3. Irene Dairy Farm
4. South African Airforce (SAAF) Museum
5. Willow Feather Farm

1 Acrobranch
www.acrobranch.co.za

5/5
Party venue rating

0/5
Rainy day option

Embark on a treetop experience where children and adults can have a unique adventure as they move from tree to tree in lush, green forests. Each course is carefully designed with a variety of obstacles, including zip lines, Tarzan swings, nets and bridges, which gradually take you from tree to tree. The staff will kit you out in a harness. When you're ready, it will be time for a training session before you move through the canopy of trees, manoeuvring your way with the swings and bridges. Afterwards you can relax in the restaurant. They also do children's birthday parties.

Tel number	012 940 1972
Address	Glen Road, Olifantsfontein
GPS marker	33°51'34"S; 22°40'28"E
Opening hours	9am–5pm daily
Most appropriate age group	3+
Pram/wheelchair-friendly	No
Baby-changing facility	No
Nearest hospital	Unitas Hospital, 012 677 8000

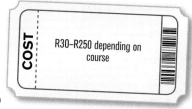
COST
R30–R250 depending on course

Nearby

Play/do: The Big Red Barn, 7 Nelson Road, Sunlawns AH, Olifantsfontein, 078 343 6939. StokeCity WakePark, Olifantsfontein Road, Midrand, 011 314 3589.

Take note:
Wear closed shoes with good tread, and dress in clothes you can move freely in (touch your toes, stretch for a tree a little out of reach, sit comfortably). Finally, people with long hair should tie it up out of the way.

2 Glen Austin Bird Sanctuary

0/5
Party venue rating

0/5
Rainy day option

Many bird species are protected in the sanctuary's beautiful, natural surroundings. Bird lovers can take their binoculars and bird books to spot and identify one of almost 200 bird species, including the malachite kingfisher and the blue crane. The sanctuary is now also a bullfrog reserve. This is a peaceful retreat on the doorstep of city dwellers who want to get away into nature.

Address	Glen Austin AH, Midrand
GPS marker	25°58'36"S; 28°10'00"E
Most appropriate age group	5+
Pram/wheelchair-friendly	No
Baby-changing facility	No
Nearest hospital	Life Carstenhof Clinic, 011 655 5500

Take note:
Horse riding is very popular in the Glen Austin area. Glen Austin Stables has horses for leasing and baiting (082 705 0538).

Nearby

Visit/see: The South African Mint Company, Panarottis Gateway Park, Old Johannesburg Road, Gateway, Centurion, 012 677 2777.

Play/do: Bounce Inc, Waterfall Corner, Waterfall Lifestyle Estate, Midrand, 011 257 2500.

Eat: Purple Cow, ground floor, Midfield Clubhouse, Midway Boulevard, Midstream, 072 128 9374. Ga Rouge Restaurant, 1795 Stonehedge Road, Candlewoods Country Estate, Centurion, 079 432 5795.

Shop: Square@Midstream, Midstream Estate.

Sleep: Ipe Tombe Guest Lodge, 63 King Willow Crescent, Midrand, 011 314 5829.

3 Irene Dairy Farm
www.irenefarm.co.za

5/5 Party venue rating
2/5 Rainy day option

This old-style, storybook farm has been kept in the same family since 1895. It has a dairy shop and is one of the last remaining places where you can still buy certified raw milk. You can also purchase cheeses, rusks and other goodies at their shop and enjoy the fair on the green lawns while the children play on the wooden jungle gyms and run around in the wide-open spaces. On this working dairy farm the cows are milked daily, and there is a special platform to enable children to experience this operation. There are two restaurants on the premises.

Take note:
The Irene Dairy Farm doesn't allow picnic baskets or blankets on their lawns.

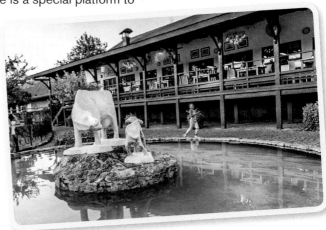

Tel number	Farm and The Deck Restaurant: 012 667 2326
	The Barn Restaurant: 012 667 4822
Address	Nellmapius Drive, Irene
GPS marker	25°52'42"S; 28°12'49"E
Closest public transport	Gautrain Centurion Station
Opening hours	Dairy shop: 8am–6pm; The Barn Restaurant: 8am–5pm;
	The Deck Restaurant: 8am–5:30pm; the farm gate closes at 6:15pm,
	by which time all guests should be out
Most appropriate age group	1+
Pram/wheelchair-friendly	Yes
Baby-changing facility	Yes
Nearest hospital	Intercare Irene Medical and Dental Centre, 012 685 5500

Nearby

Visit/see: Irene Village Theatre, 1 Pioneer Road, Irene, 082 423 0603, 084 804 0490. Smuts House Museum, Jan Smuts Avenue, Centurion, 012 667 1180. Irene Village Market, Jan Smuts Lane, 012 667 1659.

Eat: Ouma's Tea Garden, Jan Smuts Avenue, Centurion, 012 667 1176.

Shop: Irene Village Mall, Nellmapius Drive, Centurion, 012 662 4446.

Special event

The Irene Village Market has 250 unique arts and crafts stalls, an antiques and collectables section, a new deli and food stall section and children's entertainment. It runs every first and last Saturday of the month (9am–2pm) and is on the grounds of the Smuts House Museum.

---

4 South African Air Force (SAAF) Museum

www.saairforce.co.za

This is the largest military aviation museum in South Africa and tells the exciting story of aviation development in this country. You can see a variety of aircraft and missiles as well as other historically interesting aeronautical displays. South Africa boasts a very rich aviation history and you can learn about the air force's involvement in the Berlin Airlift, the Korean War, both World Wars, and numerous other events. You can also climb into a Boeing 707 and tour the cockpit. There is a gift shop selling books, model aircraft and posters, which is operated by the Friends of the SAAF Museum. All profits go towards the museum.

Take note:
Because the air force base is still in operation, you need to get clearance from the AFB Swartkop authorities to visit, but it's only a formality and part of the experience.

Tel number	012 351 9111
Address	Swartkop Airfield, Valhalla
GPS marker	25°48'30"S; 28°09'00"E
Opening hours	8:30am–4pm Wednesday to Saturday
Most appropriate age group	6+
Pram/wheelchair-friendly	Yes
Baby-changing facility	No
Nearest hospital	Unitas Hospital, 012 677 8000

Nearby

<u>Visit/see</u>: Supersport Park (cricket), 283 West Avenue, Centurion, 012 326 0560. The Centurion Society of Model Engineers, Meerpark Station, Kwikkie Crescent, Centurion, 012 643 0750. Flight of the Eagle Safaris and Tours, Wierda Park, Centurion, 012 656 0317.

<u>Play/do</u>: C'est La Vie, 270 Celliers Avenue, Centurion, 012 654 0220.

<u>Eat</u>: Isabella's, Shop 12, Eldo Square Centre, corner Volga and Willem Botha roads, Wierda Park, Eldoraigne, 082 304 4717. The Godfather, 2 Biella Centre, corner Heuwel and Mike Crawford streets, Centurion, 012 663 1859. Passi Décor and Deli, 180 Lenchen Avenue North, Lyttelton, Centurion, 012 644 0901.

<u>Shop</u>: Centurion Mall, Heuwel Street, Centurion, 012 663 1702. Forest Hill City, corner N14 and R55, Centurion, 012 007 0917.

<u>Sleep</u>: Centurion Lake Hotel, 1001 Lenchen Avenue North, Centurion, 012 643 3600. African Pride Irene Country Lodge, 391 Nellmapius Drive, 012 667 6464. Royal Elephant, Bondev Park, corner Willem Botha and Wierda roads, Eldoraigne, Centurion, 012 658 8000.

<u>For parents</u>: Elephants and Friends, Logan Avenue, Centurion, 012 665 5662.

Special event

The SAAF Museum Air Show is an award-winning, annual event that attracts up to 35,000 people. Enjoy a wide variety of delicious food stalls, spectacular displays of aerobatics, parachute drops, pyrotechnics and more.

---

5 Willow Feather Farm
www.willowfeather.co.za

Essentially a nursery, this beautiful farm also offers a tea garden and animal farm. They have a large established garden where children can run and play while parents shop at the nursery. The farmyard has sheep, pot-bellied pigs, swans and more. You can order a picnic basket to enjoy at this serene setting, or visit the tea garden. They also offer children's birthday parties.

COST
Tea garden and farmyard
R10 entry

Tel number	072 219 4831, 076 070 7015, 072 595 9342
Address	Portion 7, Doornkloof, Rietvleidam, Irene
GPS marker	25°53'05"S; 28°15'25"E
Opening hours	Nursery, tea garden and farmyard: 8am–5pm daily
Most appropriate age group	1+
Pram/wheelchair-friendly	Yes
Baby-changing facility	Yes
Nearest hospital	Intercare Irene Medical and Dental Centre, 012 685 5500

Nearby

Play/do: Rietvlei Nature Reserve and Rietvlei Dam, Game Reserve Avenue, Rietvlei, Irene, 012 358 1810.
Eat: Rietvlei Coffee Shop, in the Rietvlei Nature Reserve, 082 500 4422.
Stone Cradle, Plot 72, Game Reserve Road, Doornfontein, Rietvlei, 073 266 2555.
Sleep: Pheasant Hill, Sterkfontein Avenue, Rietvlei, 012 941 1724.

Take note:
Picnic baskets must be booked two days in advance. They do supply picnic blankets, but you can bring your own. Even if you book a picnic or party, you still need to pay the R10 conservation fee at the entrance.

Outskirts of Pretoria

1 Ann van Dyk Cheetah Centre
2 Bill Harrop's Original Balloon Safaris
3 Bush Babies Monkey Sanctuary
4 Chameleon Village
5 Cullinan Diamond Tours
6 Hennops Pride
7 Nan Hua Buddhist Temple
8 The Elephant Sanctuary

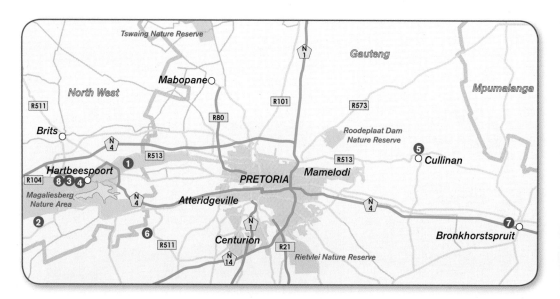

1 Ann van Dyk Cheetah Centre

www.dewildt.co.za

The mission of the centre is to ensure the long-term survival of cheetah and other animals. They breed rare and endangered species, promote public awareness (especially among the younger generation), and are fully committed to conservation and research. Visitors can enjoy a three-hour guided tour, including a touch experience. On booking, you can watch the popular 'cheetah run'.

Tel number	012 504 9906/7/8, 083 892 0515
Address	R513, Pretoria North, Farm 22
GPS marker	25°40'41"S; 27°55'26"E
Opening hours	Three-hour guided tour and touch experience: 8:30am–11:30am Monday, Wednesday and Friday and 1:30pm–4:30pm daily; two-hour family tours (only for families with young children): 9:30am and 2:30pm daily; feeding rounds: 8am Tuesday, Wednesday and Thursday
Most appropriate age group	3+
Pram/wheelchair-friendly	No
Baby-changing facility	No
Nearest hospital	Mediclinic Brits, 012 252 8000

Nearby

<u>Visit/see</u>: Inyoni Estate Crocodile Farm, Plot K108, Silkaatsnek, District Brits, 082 857 1548, 079 337 9381. Pretville, R511, Hartbeespoort, 083 266 8567. Lesedi African Lodge and Cultural Village, R512, Broederstroom, 012 205 1395.

<u>Play/do</u>: Hartbeespoort Resort, 445 JQ portion 5, Old Rustenburg Road, Hartbeespoort, 012 200 9902. Harties Cableway, R511, Plot 3, Melodie Agricultural Holdings, Hartbeespoort, 012 253 9910. Pelinduna Adventures, 138 Lanseria Road, Kalkheuwel/Hartbeespoortdam, Broederstroom, 083 286 8716.

<u>Eat</u>: The Windmill, Ifafi, Hartbeespoort, 082 578 4847.

<u>Shop</u>: Welwitschia Country Market, on R104, before Chameleon Village, 083 302 8085. Monate Sitruskelder, Damdoryn, Hartbeespoort, 012 258 3002.

<u>Sleep</u>: Glen Afric Lodge, 144 Hartbeespoort, 012 205 1412.

Take note:
The Cheetah Lodge offers accommodation on the foothills of the Magaliesberg range, with stunning views of African sunsets.

COST Three-hour tour-and-touch experience: adults R420, children 6–12 years old R220 on Tuesday, Thursday, Saturday and Sunday mornings; adults R320 and children 6–12 years old R160 on Monday, Wednesday and Friday 8:30am–11:30pm; family tours: adults R220 and children under 5 years old R100

2 Bill Harrop's Original Balloon Safaris

www.balloon.co.za

You can book different balloon tours over the Cradle of Humankind and the Magaliesberg range area in Gauteng, which boasts some of the best balloon-flying weather in South Africa. The qualified pilots have won five aviation safety awards, as well as tourism awards. You can observe the flora and fauna of the World Heritage Waterberg Biosphere from the slowly drifting vantage point of your hot-air balloon. Afterwards you can enjoy breakfast at the Clubhouse Pavilion and Restaurant. There is also a game-viewing option over the Mabula Game Lodge. Some packages include a champagne breakfast.

Tel number	011 705 3201, 083 443 2661, 083 443 2662, 083 379 5296
Address	R560, Magalies River Valley, Cradle of Humankind
GPS marker	25°49'01"S; 27°44'22"E
Closest public transport	Minibus transfers from various hotels can be arranged at an extra cost
Opening hours	Early morning daily for sunrise views
Most appropriate age group	7+
Pram/wheelchair-friendly	Yes
Baby-changing facility	No
Nearest hospital	Mediclinic Brits, 012 252 8000

Nearby
Eat: Munch Café, Garden Shop, 93 Bram Fischer Drive, 086 911 3965.
Shop: Bryanston Organic and Natural Market, 40 Culross Road, Bryanston, 011 706 3671.

COST
Magalies River Valley rates: 60-minute flight: regular R2,150, six or more people R2,040 per person, 12 or more people R1,990 per person, 24 or more people R1,935 per person

Take note:
You should be nimble enough to be able to jump unassisted from a height of 60cm and stand for the duration of the flight. Clothing should be warm enough for the chilly early morning, but should be removable because the sun can get hot. Wear comfortable shoes – no high heels.

3 Bush Babies Monkey Sanctuary

www.monkeysanctuary.co.za

0/5 Party venue rating

2/5 Rainy day option

The sanctuary is situated in a kloof in the Magaliesberg mountain range. It is one of only eight free-release primate sanctuaries in the world where monkeys enjoy freedom in natural surroundings. All tours are structured and guided as they have a strict policy of 'no human-animal interaction'. Tours are informative and take you on a leisurely stroll through natural indigenous forests on elevated wooden walkways. Afterwards you can enjoy a light lunch at the coffee bar or a prepacked picnic. They also have a curio shop for souvenirs. All proceeds go towards the sanctuary.

Tel number	012 258 9908, 071 791 7712
Address	R104, Hartbeespoort
GPS marker	25°43'11"S; 27°48'54"E
Opening hours	9am–4pm daily; tours are 75 minutes long; the last tour starts at 4pm
Most appropriate age group	1+
Pram/wheelchair-friendly	No
Baby-changing facility	No
Nearest hospital	Mediclinic Brits, 012 252 8000

Take note:
You are not allowed to feed the monkeys, as they are encouraged to hunt and search for food themselves, and not be dependent on humans.

COST: Adults R250, pensioners R195, children 4–14 years old R155; school groups: primary school children R80, high school children R90, teachers R110 and accompanying adults R130

4 Chameleon Village

www.chameleonvillage.co.za

0/5 Party venue rating

3/5 Rainy day option

Two kilometres from the Hartbeespoort Dam wall lies this quaint little village where you can shop for African curios from 150 stalls, buy up-market goodies at one of the boutique stores and visit the craft market or the Outdoor and Adventure Centre with its reptile conservation park and marimba drumming shows. There are five restaurants at the village, including Woody's Family Grill and the Chameleon Brewhouse. Also make time to visit the lion park.

Tel number	082 930 1799
Address	2km west of the Hartbeespoort Dam wall on the R104
GPS marker	25°43'36"S; 27°49'36"E
Opening hours	8am–5pm daily
Most appropriate age group	1+
Pram/wheelchair-friendly	Yes
Baby-changing facility	Yes
Nearest hospital	Mediclinic Brits, 012 252 8000

Special event

In March each year the popular Om die Dam Ultramarathon takes place. Dubbed as one of the most scenic marathons in the country, this 50km race is not for the unfit. There is also a 10km race and a 5km fun run.

COST: Free entry to the village; Chameleon Village Lion Park: adults R100, children 5–10 years old R50, children under 5 free; Reptile and Conservation Park and Rhythm Africa Marimba Group: call to enquire

Take note: There is loads for children to do: jumping castles, activities and playgrounds.

---

5 **Cullinan Diamond Tours**
www.diamondtourscullinan.co.za

 0/5 Party venue rating

 3/5 Rainy day option

The Cullinan Diamond Pipe is the oldest of its kind in the world. Surface tours of the mine last between 90 minutes and two hours. You can watch an introductory DVD of the underground operations before visiting the Diamond Display Room where there are replicas of the most famous diamonds on the planet. You can also enter a mock-up of a life-size underground tunnel and visit the winding engine room, which is the heart of the operation. You have the opportunity at the lookout point to see the Big Hole, where a volcanic eruption took place 1.2 billion years ago. End the tour with a visit to the Diamond Cutting and Jewellery Shop where you can buy a souvenir. Bookings for tours are essential.

Tel number	012 734 0081, 083 261 0082
Address	1 Bank Street, Cullinan
GPS marker	28°40'17"S; 28°30'59"E
Opening hours	Tours at 10:30am and 2pm Monday to Friday; 10:30am and 12pm Saturday and Sunday
Most appropriate age group	10+
Pram/wheelchair-friendly	No
Baby-changing facility	No
Nearest hospital	In Pretoria

Take note: No children under 16 years of age are allowed to go on tours down the mine shafts.

Nearby

Visit/see: Oak Avenue Boulevard, Cullinan.

Play/do: Cullinan Adventure Zone, on the R513 and Olievenhout Road, Cullinan, 012 734 0507. Diamond X Cowboy Ranch, Farm Grootfontein, Rayton, Cullinan, 082 410 3180.

Eat: The Hearts of Coffee and Gift Shop, Cullinan Junction, Hotel Street, 084 579 1803. The Lemon Tree Garden Restaurant, 95 Oak Avenue, 012 734 0778. Oppistasie Restaurant and Steak House, on the platform at the station, 071 659 2180 or 083 570 8291.

Sleep: Butjani Lodge, Portion 7 Leeudraai Farm, Cullinan, 082 803 8608.

Special events

Every two months on a Sunday morning, Friends of the Rail organise train trips from Hermanstad Station in Pretoria to Cullinan (www.friendsofthe rail.com). The Mother's Day Vintage Train to Cullinan is also very popular.

COST — Diamond tours R120

---

6 # Hennops Pride
www.hennopspride.caravanparks.co.za

3/5 Party venue rating   **0/5** Rainy day option

Hennops Pride is a natural paradise in the Schurveberg, which is situated on the banks of the Hennops River. You can stay over in a chalet or camp, and day visitors are welcome to enjoy a picnic or a braai. There are six swimming pools, including a splash pool for little ones, as well as a playground for children. Activities include fishing, mountain biking, scenic walking trails, 4x4 trails, trampolines, putt putt and volleyball courts.

Tel number	083 288 9915
Address	R511, Fourways/Hartbeespoort Road, Hennops River
GPS marker	25°50'19"S; 27°58'32"E
Opening hours	9am–6pm for day visitors
Most appropriate age group	1+
Pram/wheelchair-friendly	No
Baby-changing facility	Yes
Nearest hospital	Mediclinic Brits, 012 252 8000

COST — Day rates: adults R80, children 0–14 years old R20, pensioners R60, R20 per vehicle; 4x4 route R100

Nearby

Play/do: Hennops Adventures, R511, 082 825 9205.
Phaladingwe Nature Trail, R104, NECSA Road (Old Pelindaba Road),
Preller House, Broederstroom, 071 352 6341.
Eat: Al Fiume Restaurant, R511, 079 531 3725.
Sleep: River Place Country Estate, R511, 079 531 3725.
La Wiida Lodge, Portion 183 of the Farm Hennopsriver, R511
William Nicol Drive, Hennopsriver Valley.

Take note:
Dogs are allowed by prior arrangement.

---

7 Nan Hua Buddhist Temple

www.nanhuatemple.org

 0/5 Party venue rating

 3/5 Rainy day option

The temple runs tours for visitors where you can see the impressive Chinese Palace gong, a replica of the original, which dates back approximately 2,000 years to the Han Dynasty in ancient China. Also view the large white Temple Lions. These are mythological animals called Dogs of Fu, the miraculous progeny of a Pekingese dog and an African lion. The tour includes a visit to the museum where you can view interesting artefacts. You can also relax in the coffee shop and browse the curio shop. The temple offers meditation retreats through-out the year.

Take note:
The Netcare hospital in Bronkhorstspruit has closed down, so be prepared to be transported to hospitals in Pretoria in case of an emergency.

COST

Temple tours are free, Sunday vegetarian lunch R30 (12pm–12:30pm)

Tel number	013 931 0009
Address	27 Nan Hua Road, Cultura Park, Bronkhorstspruit
GPS marker	25°49'28"S; 28°44'03"E
Opening hours	9am–5pm Tuesday to Sunday
Most appropriate age group	7+
Pram/wheelchair-friendly	Yes
Baby-changing facility	No

Special event
Nan Hua Temple periodically hosts events such as the Chinese New Year Cultural Festival, Bathing the Buddha Ceremony, Ceremony of Light and Peace, and New Year's Eve Sky Lantern Offering Ceremony

The Elephant Sanctuary
www.elephantsanctuary.co.za

 0/5 Party venue rating

 3/5 Rainy day option

The African elephants at the sanctuary have been domesticated through positive reinforcement animal management principles, which means you can interact with them. Enjoy the opportunity to touch, feed and get to know these beasts on guided tours. You can also walk trunk-in-hand with them. Guides provide in-depth information and insight into the elephants. You can meet them in the forest area, visit their stables and on hot days you might even catch them taking a swim. Elephant-back riding is optional. Afterwards you can enjoy a drink on the deck overlooking the elephant boma and shop for souvenirs.

COST Elephant interaction: adults R650, children 4–14 years old R270; elephant-back riding: adults R465, children 8–14 years old R275

Tel number	012 258 9904, 012 258 9905/6/7
Address	R104, Hartbeespoort
GPS marker	25°43'18"S; 27°48'27"E
Opening hours	Elephant interaction 8am, 10am and 2pm daily – programmes run for approximately two hours; elephant-back riding on booking
Most appropriate age group	4+
Pram/wheelchair-friendly	No
Baby-changing facility	No
Nearest hospital	Mediclinic Brits, 012 252 8000

Special event
An overnight experience includes sleeping in a 10-bed lodge, which shares a wall with the elephant stables. Children of all ages are welcome on this experience.

Take note:
The Elephant Sanctuary and Bush Babies Monkey Sanctuary are now on the same property – make a weekend of it and visit both venues.

My Favourite Venues

Place	Date	Comments

Party Planning Guide

Occasion

Guest list

Theme

Place

Date and time

Catering

Other

First edition published in 2015 by MapStudio™ South Africa

ISBN (Print) 978-1-77026-696-4
ISBN (ePdf) 978-1-77026-755-8

Production Manager John Loubser
Project Manager Genené Hart
Editor Thea Grobbelaar
Designer Nicole Bannister
Cartographers Nicole Bannister, Genené Hart
Proofreader Joy Clack
Reproduction Resolution, Cape Town
Marketing marketing@mapstudio.co.za
Feedback research@mapstudio.co.za
Photo credits © 2015 Images as credited below:
Shaen Adey, pp8, 9(top), 10–15, 17–23, 25, 28–31, 34–39 (top), 41–43, 44 (bottom), 45, 48, 54–56 (top), 58, 59 (top), 60, 61, 63, 64 (bottom), 66, 68, 69, 71–73, 75, 76, 79, 80 (top), 82, 85; Africa Whispers, p80 (bottom); Artscape, p39 (bottom); Nicole Bannister, pp50 (top), 59 (bottom); Carina Beyer/Iziko Natural History Museum, p16; Blasters, p47 (top); Blue Rock, p53; Cape Town Science Centre, p32; Cape Town Zipline Tours, p33 (top); City Rock Indoor Climbing, p33 (bottom); Crocworld Conservation Centre, p77; CROW, 64 (top); Galleria Ice Rink, p78; Giba Gorge MTB Park, p81; Skye Grove, p57; Genené Hart, pp24, 47 (bottom), 49, 50 (bottom); Graceland Venues, p56 (bottom); Karkloof Canopy Tours, p83; KZN Sharks Board, p74; Lucky Bean, p84; Moses Mabhida Stadium, p67; Phezulu Safari Park, p86; Peter Primich, p89–171; SunScene Outdoor Adventure Course, p44 (top); The White House Stables, p51; uShaka Marine World, p70; Winsome View Animal Farm, p87; YoungBlood Collective, p9 (top); Zip Zap Circus, p28.
Cover photography © 2015 (clockwise from top left): Delfina de Faria; Two Oceans Aquarium; Cape Town Science Centre; Son Surf - Jami van der Merwe; Spree - Neil Roberts Mayne; Bounce Inc; City Sightseeing South Africa - Justin Lee; Yvette Dreyer-Ferreira; Montecasino Bird Gardens; Orlando Towers; Thule Group; Acrobranch Adventure Park.
Printed and bound by CTP Printers, Cape Town
eBook available from www.mapstudio.co.za and major online retailers

MapStudio™
Unit 3, Block B, M5 Park, Eastman Road,
Maitland, 7405
PO Box 193, Maitland, 7404
Tel: 0860 10 50 50
www.mapstudio.co.za

Maps © 2015 MapStudio™
© MapStudio™ 2015

Check out all our websites
www.mapstudio.co.za
www.globetrottertravelguides.com

Purchase our iPhone and iPad app
www.parkspotterafrica.com

Check out our digital offerings
www.myroute.co.za

Quality MAPS SINCE 1958

Buy our ebooks at www.mapstudio.co.za or www.globetrottertravelguides.com